The Luminous Web

The
Luminous Web

Essays on Science and Religion

Barbara Brown
Taylor

COWLEY PUBLICATIONS
Cambridge · Boston
Massachusetts

Published in the United States of America by Cowley
Publications, a division of the Society of St. John the
Evangelist. No portion of this book may be reproduced, stored
in or introduced into a retrieval system, or transmitted, in
any form or by any means — including photocopying — without
the prior written permission of Cowley Publications, except
in the case of brief quotations embodied in critical articles
and reviews.

Library of Congress Cataloging-in-Publication Data
Taylor, Barbara Brown.
    The luminous web : essays on science and religion /
    by Barbara Brown Taylor.
        p.   cm.
    Includes bibliographical references.
    ISBN 1--56101-169-X (alk. paper)
    1. Religion and science. I. Title.
    BL240.2 .T29 2000
    261.5'5 — dc21   99-057233

An earlier version of Chapter 2 appeared in *The Princeton
Seminary Bulletin* (New Series 1999). An earlier version of
Chapter 3 appeared in *The Christian Century* (June 2-9, 1999)
and a portion of Chapter 4 first appeared in *The Habersham
Review* (Autumn 1998). The author wishes to thank the edi-
tors and readers of these publications for their support.

Cynthia Shattuck, editor; Vicki Black, copyeditor and
designer

This book was printed in the United States of America on
recycled, acid-free paper.

Cowley Publications
28 Temple Place • Boston, Massachusetts 02111
800-225-1534 • www.cowley.org

TO EDWARD,
my closest kin and most trusted advisor

Contents

Acknowledgments

I want to thank Thomas Gillespie and the faculty of Princeton Theological Seminary for inviting me to give the 1998 Macleod Lectures on Preaching, which provided the impetus for this book. The careful questions I was asked at Princeton helped me revise the material for a more general audience at Mercer University, where Walter Shurden kindly asked me to deliver the Harry Vaughn Smith Lectures in 1999. Again, the responses I received sharpened my thinking. I am particularly grateful to Steve Runholt, Peter del Nagro, Tom McMullen, Lee Adams Young, and Rollin Armour, Sr., who wrote me with suggestions for fine-tuning portions of this book; to Howard E. Johnson and Rick Austin, who allowed me to tell their stories; and to Peter Hawkins, who gave me the conclusion to chapter two.

My thanks go also to David Heim, editor of *The Christian Century*, who agreed to publish one chapter of this work last spring. Among the many responses I received to that article was a letter from Louis Jensen, who did me the great courtesy of critiquing it from one scientist's point of view. His fidelity to facts and to precision in language provided me with one of my most valuable lessons in the dialogue between religion and science. Needless to say, neither he nor any of my other correspondents bears any responsibility for errors I may have made in these pages.

I am also grateful to my editors Cynthia Shattuck and Vicki Black for grooming the manuscript over and over again, and to Denise Bobo for typing it. My deepest thanks are reserved for my husband Ed. When deadlines loomed and I lost all confidence in what I was doing, he talked me through the night. For this and for other gifts too many to count, I thank him.

BARBARA BROWN TAYLOR
CLARKESVILLE, GEORGIA

x

I

Between Science and Faith

Religion declined not because it was refuted, but because it became irrelevant, dull, oppressive, insipid. When faith is completely replaced by creed, worship by discipline, love by habit; when the crisis of today is ignored because of the splendor of the past; when faith becomes an heirloom rather than a living fountain; when religion speaks only in the name of authority rather than with the voice of compassion, its message becomes meaningless.

ABRAHAM HESCHEL

I am not a scientist. It is true that I received a small microscope for my ninth birthday and gave myself headaches by looking into it for hours at a time. The first thing I saw was a hair plucked from my own head, as fat and shiny as a tarred telephone pole. After that, I tried everything that would fit below the eyepiece: flower petals, dirt, a page torn from the telephone book. I spent the better part of an afternoon with a dropper full of pond water, and—once I had worked up my nerve—with a smear of my own blood that was as beautiful to me as a red stained glass window.

The next year there was a chemistry set, with all the requisite explosions, followed by an electromagnetic device that made all the hairs on my arm stand up. When my fifth-grade science class studied genetics, I went to the pet store and bought a dozen mice. Half of them were white with pink eyes. The other half had dark fur and black eyes. My project was to breed a white mouse with black eyes, or—if that turned out to be impossible—then at least to produce a dark mouse with pink eyes.

I do not remember whether or not I succeeded, but I do remember that I midwifed quite a lot of mice. There were the inevitable mutants, including a small white mouse that did nothing but turn round and round in tiny circles all day, and a mother mouse who ate each of her newborn babies in turn. By the time it was all over, there was a small colony of escapees who lived in the basement and one lone fugitive who somehow got loose in the family car. We never saw him, but sometimes we could hear him chewing the upholstery inside the seats, and once we found a little nest he had made in the trunk.

After I arrived at high school, my interest in science waned. When I balked at dissecting the same kind of mice I had spent months breeding, a classmate helpfully explained the problem to me. In the first place, he said, I was a girl, and girls were notoriously bad at science. In the second place, he said, I made A's in English, which was a sure sign that my mind was tuned more to words than to mice. His advice was that I should save myself a lot of grief by steering clear of science altogether. What use would someone like me ever have for logarithms or the periodic table?

Taking his advice, I avoided math and all the other sciences along with it, which meant that I did not see much more of him. I spent my time with the editors of the school literary magazine, who wrote poetry and read Kafka. When we walked by the chemistry lab we held our breath, to avoid inhaling sulfurous fumes. As far as we were concerned, we were as different from the people inside as birds were from bats. I cannot remember anyone in high school who violated this academic caste system. If you belonged to the Drama Club, you did not join the Science Club. If you were good at trigonometry, you assumed you would never understand the allegory in *Moby Dick*.

5

The Standardized Achievement Test I took in my junior year confirmed these divisions. The math part of my brain and the verbal part of my brain were apparently so alien to one another that they required different tests and earned different scores. I deduced that I did not possess one intelligence but two—one a Ford and one a Ferrari—both housed in the same garage. I drove off to college with this schizophrenia intact and continued the pattern I had begun in high school. I satisfied my science requirement with a course in geology, sleeping well at night while my roommate wrestled the angels of organic chemistry.

When I became a religion major, I learned from my professors that science and religion were two very different things. Science dealt with the physical world. It was interested in how things worked and preferred things that worked the same way every time. Once a physical body passed the test of predictability, it was awarded an equation that described its behavior, freeing science to move on to the next frontier. Science was objective. Science dealt with facts. Science had incredibly useful things to show for its efforts, such as vaccines, light bulbs, x-rays, and computers.

Religion, on the other hand, dealt with the spiritual world. It was less interested in how things worked
than in what they meant and how human beings
should behave in relationship to them. Since the spiritual dimension transcended the merely physical, it
could not be described in predictable equations.
Religion was subjective. Religion dealt with values,
and while it had its own useful things to show, such
as schools, hospitals, churches, and synagogues,
these rarely made the headlines unless something
went wrong.

In this manner, I learned that my being was divided in yet another way. Not only was my mind divided into the (woefully inadequate) mathematical part
and the (much more promising) verbal part measured
by the SAT, but my entire being was also divided into
the physical part that I could see in the mirror every
morning and the spiritual part that no one but God
could really see. This latter division between body
and soul seemed to apply to the whole wide world as
well. There was matter and there was spirit, I was
taught, but they were not the same thing.

As soon as I decided to go to seminary, science
dropped off my radar screen altogether. As an
ordained minister, I would not be required to deal in
precise measurements or verifiable facts. I would deal
in meaning, faith, morality, love—all those invisible
things that cannot be seen through a microscope or
mounted on a pin. Plus, knowledge is pretty safely
compartmentalized at the graduate level. While a few
of my higher-achieving classmates took ethics classes
at the medical school or dabbled in environmental

law, most of us never left the divinity quadrangle, where our pleasant days were marked by the tolling of the bell in the chapel tower.

Later, when I was a hospital chaplain, I learned about "the God of the gaps." While I certainly paid calls on patients facing nothing more serious than a gall bladder operation, the calls I remember best are the ones that came in the middle of the night. By the time my beeper went off, the family had already been called at home and told that the patient had "taken a turn for the worse." That meant the patient had died, but since hospital policy required a doctor to deliver the news, the other language was used (with the additional hope that people might drive more carefully if they did not know the truth).

The designated meeting place was called "the family room" — a dreadful name, since it was really the room where families fell apart. I waited with them until the doctor arrived, and then I stepped out into the hall. At the moment I cannot tell you why I did that. Maybe it was because, in many cases, the family knew the doctor much better than they knew me and I wanted to allow them their privacy. Or maybe it was because I found it so hard to watch a doctor already sick with failure face the fury of grieving relatives.

Most doctors did not stay very long. Their jobs, after all, were over. When we passed each other in the doorway of the family room wearing the badges of our offices — one of us with a stethoscope and the other with a Bible — we might as well have passed a baton. Science had gone as far as it could go. It was religion's turn to step into the breach.

Strangely or not, that is where I have felt most useful in my life—at the point where all the things that are supposed to work do not work anymore and people are faced with the vast mystery of being. I have never felt compelled to solve most mysteries, which may be another reason why I am not a scientist. I cannot prove most of the things that give me life. I cannot generate statistics on the value of truth, kindness, or beauty. I cannot document my theory that food eaten with someone else tastes better than food that is eaten alone, or that the surprising sound of Canada geese overhead can do more to restore hope than five hours of good psychotherapy.

Because I am a believer and not a scientist, I cannot assert that such things are true. I can only assert that they are "true for me," which lacks the pleasing ring of authority. Perhaps this is why religious people are so delighted when articles on the efficacy of prayer show up in medical journals. Who could hope for more authority than that? It is a telling sign of our times that the phrase "Scientific studies show..." carries more weight than "Thus says the Lord...."

An historian of science might say that the story I have just told you is a microcosm of the human story as a whole. In the ancient world, religion and science were little more than two ways of being curious. The truths each of them told were assumed to be divine truths. The world was not yet split into "sacred" and "secular" realms. The definitive divorce came in the sixteenth century, when Copernicus guessed that the earth circled the sun instead of vice versa.

For the first time, the truth that could be observed in the real world conflicted with the truth revealed by God in scripture. Copernicus and the Bible could not both be right about the placement of the planets, and the scientific revolution began. The church stuck by the Bible, condemning both Copernicus and Galileo as heretics. The scientific community drew away from the church, choosing truth they could see over truth they could not. When the astronomer Pierre de Laplace explained nature as a self-sufficient mechanism, the Emperor Napoleon asked him where that left God. "I have no need of that hypothesis," Laplace replied.[1]

Ever since then, it seems, science and religion have been engaged in a head-butting match. Science accuses religion of superstition and hyperbole; religion accuses science of nihilism and amorality. At issue are their different perspectives on truth, and in particular their disagreement about whether or not creation shows evidence of some supreme will at work. Just lately I have been watching the battle take place on automobile bumpers in the rural south, where I live. First there was the silver fish emblem, meant to let me know that the driver of the car ahead of me was a Christian. Given the way some of these people drove, I am not sure the advertisement was really a good idea.

Sometimes the fish was just a fish and sometimes it contained the name "Jesus." Then came the silver fish emblem with two little feet added to it and the name "Darwin" inside. I assumed this either meant that the driver in the car ahead of me was not a Christian, or was a Christian evolutionist. At any rate, these new emblems rarely coincided with bumper stickers warning me that in case of the rapture the driver of the car would disappear.

Now I am seeing a third emblem: a great big silver fish with its mouth wide open, gobbling up the little silver fish with feet. The little fish still says "Darwin" inside, while the big fish says "Truth." This would be funnier if the battle were confined to automobile bumpers, but unfortunately it is not. One of my colleagues, who is both a church-going Southern Baptist and a professor of evolutionary biology, remembers being attacked from both sides while he was earning his Ph.D. With notable exceptions, his church family disowned him for teaching science that contradicted the Bible, while his scientific community scorned him for believing in God.

While I know of no poll reporting how many religious people believe also in science, *Scientific American* recently published the results of a survey on how many American scientists believe also in God. The researchers, Edward J. Larson and Larry Witham, did their best to replicate a survey carried out in 1914 and again in 1933 by a professor of psychology at Bryn Mawr College named James H. Leuba. Basing his survey on two beliefs he considered central to Christianity—a God influenced by prayer, and an afterlife—Leuba found that four out of ten scientists believed in God as defined in his survey. In the second part of his survey, he polled the scientific elite—

people who were listed in *American Men of Science* with stars by their names — among whom he found much higher levels of disbelief.

All these years later, the figures hold steady. According to Larson and Witham's surveys in 1996 and 1998, four out of ten "lesser" scientists still believe in God, while only one out of ten "greater" scientists professes belief. Since the standard reference work (now called *American Men and Women Scientists*) no longer stars entries, Larson and Witham surveyed members of the elite National Academy of Sciences. They found NAS biologists to be the most skeptical of religion, with ninety-five percent of respondents claiming atheism or agnosticism, and NAS mathematicians to be the most receptive, with one out of six expressing belief in a personal God.[2]

These results defy Leuba's prediction that religious disbelief would grow both among American scientists and Americans in general. But they support the widely perceived division between people of science and people of faith. In 1981, when the NAS was concerned about public opinion in the wake of the decisions by two states to mandate equal time for "creation science" in public school biology classes, the Academy adopted this policy statement: "Religion and science are separate and mutually exclusive realms of human thought whose presentation in the same context leads to misunderstanding of both scientific theory and religious belief."[3]

The "mutually exclusive" phrase is the one that worries me, given the dualism that has dogged me all my life. As I have said, I grew up thinking of reality

not as one but two. First there is physical reality —
first because it is the one you can see and touch —
which depends on science for everything from
medicine to e-mail. Then there is spiritual reality —
beyond sight and touch — which depends entirely on
God. The first reality relies on reason, which wants to
know how gravity works and why plants grow. The
other reality relies on faith, which knows it will never
find answers to all its questions. The first reality is
governed by discernible laws of physics, while the
second is governed by the inscrutable will of God.

But if God is one, then how can reality be two? If
God is the origin of all that is — earth, moon, and stars,
as well as spirit, soul, and consciousness, then how
can science (which means to tell me the truth about
physical reality) and religion (which means to tell me
the truth about spiritual reality) be enemies? And
why should living my life require me to use two different operating manuals? If God is truly one and
truly God of all, then how can truth be divided?

Those are the kinds of questions that led me to
start reading science again, almost ten years ago now.
No one I know was very interested in science until
the publication of Stephen Hawking's book *A Brief
History of Time* in 1988. There were certainly other
books about science written for popular audiences
before that — most notably, Gary Zukav's book *The
Dancing Wu Li Masters,* published in 1979. But while
Zukav's book remained something of a cult classic
among the readers I knew, Hawking's book soon
showed up on coffee tables all over town. According
to my informal survey, many more people bought the

book than ever actually read it, but what struck me
was the enormous interest it provoked.

Maybe it was the author himself who captured people's imaginations—diminutive Stephen Hawking
propped in a wheelchair, his fragile body wasted by
Lou Gehrig's disease while his robust mind roamed
the stars—but I think it was more than that. I think it
was also his quest for a "theory of everything" that
caught people's attention. Even those of us who did
not have a clue what that meant found ourselves
drawn to the idea. Wouldn't it be wonderful to understand everything? More to the point, wouldn't it be
wonderful to discover the unity at the heart of all
diversity—a theory that would tie everything together
instead of driving them further and further apart?

"If we do discover a complete theory," Hawking
wrote in the final paragraph of his book, "it should in
time be understandable in broad principle by everyone, not just a few scientists. Then we shall all,
philosophers, scientists, and just ordinary people, be
able to take part in the discussion of why it is that we
and the universe exist. If we find the answer to that,
it would be the ultimate triumph of human reason—
for then we would truly know the mind of God."[4]

Ten years later, Edward O. Wilson put forth his
own theory of everything in another best-selling book
called *Consilience: The Unity of Knowledge.* He came at
his subject from the perspective of sociobiology
instead of physics, but his vision was similar. Calling
the humanities, social sciences, and natural sciences
out of their intellectual isolationism, he argued that a

unity of knowledge is both possible and necessary if we are to save the planet.

My project in these pages is much less grand. At this point in my thinking, I do not believe that religion and science can or should be reconciled. Their methods, their interests and their ways of knowing things are too different for that. They are two distinct ways of looking at the world, and each has its own beauties and virtues. When they invade each other's territory, damage is generally done — as when religionists decide that evolution and big bang theory are not essential to public school curricula, or when scientists liken belief in God to belief in fairies.

What I want to challenge in these pages is the presumed enmity between the two, especially in an age when their dialogue is more vital than ever. Many of us grew up on the classical distinction between science as the study of how the world works and religion as the study of why we are here and how we should behave, but this boundary is eroding as science advances into areas that were once the exclusive domain of religion. Pick up a scientific journal today and you are likely to see at least one article on the creation of the universe, the origin of life, the nature of consciousness, or the destiny of the cosmos. Meanwhile, scientific discoveries in the areas of cloning, genetic engineering, and artificial intelligence are raising huge ethical questions for humankind. Does our ability to do a thing also grant us warrant to do it? If we find that we *can* make a human being, does that necessarily mean that we *should?*

14

While most of the impetus for dialogue these days seems to be coming from the religious side, there are indications that the scientific side has some questions too. Four years ago, a resident theologian named Anne Foerst joined the staff of the Artificial Intelligence Laboratory at the Massachusetts Institute of Technology. Her job is to ask questions about human identity in a technological age, and especially about how smart machines may impact our sense of what it means to be human.

"I think that computer science, and especially artificial intelligence, is *the* field for religious inquiry," says Foerst, a German research scientist who holds degrees in theology as well as computer science and philosophy. To date, most artificial intelligences have been software applications such as the chess-playing IBM computer Deep Blue. But MIT lab director Rodney Brooks says that a disembodied intelligence cannot experience the world as humans do. Only through experience as a physical being can smart robots develop emotions, Brooks says, which are essential for a truly intelligent being. His brainchild, a human-shaped robot named Cog, is designed to explore and adapt to the world much as a human baby does. The aim is for Cog to become conscious of his body, his environment, and perhaps even his "self."

"At some point, Cog-like robots will be part of our community," Foerst says. If they look like us, act like us, and are aware like us, she asks, then should we not welcome them into the community of humankind? Should we not baptize them?[5]

While not everyone welcomes discussions like this one, I believe that the dialogue between science and religion offers benefits to both sides. Scientists are invited to address the deep issues of meaning and purpose that are raised by their work, while theologians are challenged to articulate a more rigorous and rational faith. I discovered the benefits first-hand in my correspondence with a retired scientist who took me to task for the way I wrote about quantum physics.

Making a distinction between physics and metaphysics, he sent me back to reread the material. "Don't assume you know what quantum physicists mean when they say something," he cautioned me. "You should try to know what *they* mean when they say it." Point by point, he walked me through the differences between the *expansion of space* and the *velocity of material through space,* between *micro* physics and *macro* physics, between *intelligent communication between particles* and *quantum entanglement.*

At first I was irritated by what I considered to be a lot of picky attention to detail. As a narrative preacher, I am used to grabbing the metaphor implicit in an event and running with it. I am concerned with the "big ideas," not the trifling facts, but as I did what my correspondent asked me to do, I experienced a kind of enlightenment. I understood what a sloppy thinker I had become, at least from a scientific point of view. I relearned the value of paying exquisite attention to detail, and to making the distinction between the facts and my interpretation of the facts. Above all, I gained a great deal of respect for the discipline required by scientific method, which will not tolerate fuzzy or wishful thinking.

I did encounter "wishful mathematics," however, in my preliminary reading on superstring theory. While there are actually five different string theories in the works, they all posit tiny invisible strings vibrating in a space-time of ten dimensions as the only known way to reconcile general relativity and quantum mechanics in the universe.[6] Since this can only be mathematically supposed and not actually demonstrated, it belongs to what is known as theoretical physics, and one thing I have discovered is that all physicists do not see eye to eye.

In retrospect, I should not have been surprised, but as a confessed fuzzy thinker I somehow idealized scientists as people who all agreed on everything. Now I have heard from a physicist who calls David Bohm and Richard Wheeler "dubious thinkers," and who suggests that scientists such as Paul Davies and Ian Barbour spend much of their time in a state called "Dreamland." The objection seems to be that these people have "gotten carried away in their imaginations," where they have confused mathematical possibilities with real experimental results. They are expressing philosophical opinions instead of reporting verifiable scientific calculations.[7]

With considerably more venom, the British zoologist Richard Dawkins takes on any physicist (including Einstein and Hawking) who lets "God" stand for "That which we don't understand." It would be a harmless trick, he says, "if it were not continually misunderstood by those hungry to misunderstand it." Meanwhile, he says, optimistic scientists will insist "That which we don't understand" means only "That which we don't *yet* understand."[8] With such arguments ringing in my ears, I am left wondering if fundamentalism and mysticism, evangelicalism and puritanism, are categories that apply to science as well as religion.

Although Albert Einstein was not a conventionally religious man, one of his most often repeated quotations is "Science without religion is lame; religion without science is blind." With hundreds of new courses on science and religion being offered each year, along with dozens of new conferences, institutes, journals and books, there is evidence that many people agree with him. Take, for instance, Robert John Russell, who—with degrees in both physics and divinity—runs the Center for Theology and the Natural Sciences in Berkeley. Or consider J. Wentzel van Huyssteen, who occupies the James I. McCord chair in Theology and Science at Princeton Theological Seminary. In July 1998, *Newsweek* magazine's cover story announced "Science Finds God," while the October 1998 issue of *Theology Today* followed suit with an issue on theology and science in conversation.

The Templeton Foundation, founded by financier-philanthropist Sir John Templeton, annually awards large cash prizes to writers and preachers in the area of science and religion. Templeton is interested in what he calls "humility theology," which emphasizes the need for both scientists and religious believers to recognize the limits in their way of knowing and leave room for the other. As American humorist Will Rogers put it, "We're all ignorant, just on different subjects."

While theologians are jumping on the religion and science bandwagon in greater numbers than scientists (perhaps because the laboratory now wields more power than the church?), humility is a virtue no scientist can live without. Unlike religion, which trades on unswerving faith in certain central doctrines, science has to remain open to its own overthrow. In order for something to be called a theory, it has to be falsifiable. Today's certainty can always become tomorrow's antique notion, which makes doubt an essential tool in the scientific investigation of reality.

Nobel laureate Richard Feynman, who was one of this century's most charismatic physicists, was a great defender of doubt. "I feel a responsibility," he wrote, "as a scientist who knows the great value of a satisfactory philosophy of ignorance, and the progress made possible by such a philosophy, progress which is the fruit of freedom of thought. I feel a responsibility to proclaim the value of this freedom and to teach that doubt is not to be feared, but that it is to be welcomed as the possibility of a new potential for human beings."9

Language like that is what keeps me reading science—not only for what it offers me personally but also for how it informs my sense of vocation. Contrary to popular opinion, theology is not a static and monolithic discipline. While it may not be as limber as science, it remains a dynamic enterprise.

Research in every area of theology, from biblical studies to ecumenism, continues to provide believers with
fuel for rethinking their positions and reformulating
their doctrines.

As more and more theologians tune in, research in
science is having the same effect. How can we speak
of human origin or destiny without taking into
account the biological mechanisms of life on earth?
How can we speak of human meaning or purpose
without pondering the actual structure of the universe? Above all, how can we continue to speak of
God in ways that lead us to live divided lives, without ever addressing the significant (and valuable) differences between religious and scientific ways of
thinking? People of faith may be excused for *wanting*
to avoid the dialogue, but not for avoiding it. Our
faith in an incarnational God will not allow us to
ignore the physical world, nor any of its nuances.

One of my correspondents, who is an engineer
married to an ordained minister, told me the story of
something that happened to him in an adult Sunday
school class. On the first Sunday of class, he said, the
associate pastor walked up to the blackboard and
wrote three words at the top of it. On the left-hand
side of the board he wrote "Religion." In the middle,
he wrote "Superstition," and on the right-hand side
he wrote "Science." My friend objected and asked if
he could rearrange the words. When the pastor said
yes, the engineer got up and erased the board. On the
left-hand side of the board he wrote "Science" directly
under "Religion." On the right-hand side he wrote
"Superstition."

20

When asked to make sense of what he had done, he replied, "Science and religion are both searches for truth and should be on the same side." Several years later, he added, he formulated what came to be one of the guiding concepts of his life. "When truth and belief come into conflict, it is better to change one's belief to fit the truth than to change the truth to fit one's belief."

The only problem with that principle is that truth comes in at least two varieties — facts and meanings — and the same facts do not always generate the same meanings. In the chapters that follow, I will knowingly violate this boundary by imposing my own meaning on scientific facts or theories. In every case, I will try to be very clear about where the science ends and my own interpretation begins, but this will still constitute a violation (as my scientific correspondents have taught me). Meanwhile, this slim book represents my own attempt at entering into a dialogue with science, with all the clumsiness associated with first steps. Some of the science in the book will be outdated by the time it appears in print. I hope that the conversation will *not* be, and that others may join me in it, trusting that the truth will set us free.

II

The Evolution of Praise

No scientific theory, including evolution, can pose any threat to religion — for these two great tools of human understanding operate in complementary (not contrary) fashion in their totally separate realms: science as an inquiry about the factual state of the natural world, religion as a search for spiritual meaning and ethical values.

STEPHEN JAY GOULD

There may be no one whose scientific discoveries did more to upset religion than Charles Robert Darwin, whose book *On the Origin of Species* appeared in 1859. Although he used the word "evolve" only once in that work—in the very last sentence—his name became synonymous with the theory of evolution. The offense lay, for people who believed in God, in its proposal that natural selection is a blind, purposeless process that operates through random variations, and that this aimless mechanism accounts for all forms of life on earth. Darwin's denial of design in nature was almost universally interpreted as a denial of the divine in nature. His self-sufficient universe, controlled only by chance and necessity, left no room for any God but a very remote and disinterested one. Cornell biologist William Provine has said that evolutionary theory is "the greatest engine of atheism ever invented."[1]

According to my colleague Rick Austin, who teaches biology at Piedmont College, evolution cannot properly be called a theory, since a theory is a hypothesis that has been repeatedly tested over time.

While there is no doubt among even the most conservative scientists that natural selection does in fact occur, it is not possible to test the hypothesis that this mechanism explains the leap from great apes to humankind. Creation is not repeatable, at least not in our lifetimes. Scientifically speaking, all of our stories about it are hypotheses, and choosing any one of them to call true is an act of faith.

One Sunday afternoon a couple of years ago, I paid a call on a ninety-three-year-old woman. She was one of those elderly people whose appearances deceive. Behind her high white forehead and her clouded-over eyes lurked a fully engaged and formidable mind. She wanted to talk about evolution, so we talked about evolution — or rather, I listened to her talk about evolution, and especially about the danger of teaching such a wrong-headed notion in public school.

"The very idea!" said this woman who was born sixteen years after Darwin died. "Can you imagine teaching children that they come from monkeys instead of from God?" I said something about how evolution itself seemed like a kind of miracle to me, but she was adamant. "You can't have it both ways," she said. "We are either here by design or we are here by chance."

The very next day I taught a class on the book of Genesis, explaining to my students how important it was for the Hebrews to put their story down on paper. This was especially true if Genesis was written in Babylon, as some scholars suppose. In the creation story of that foreign culture, the cosmos was made from the dismembered corpse of the goddess Tiamat, whose skull was split by her youngest son Marduk. By murdering his evil mother, Marduk brought order out of chaos with an act of redemptive violence.[2]

This was not the story Hebrew parents wanted their Babylonian-born children to learn in school. So they set down their own account—about a good creation made by a good God—which went a long way toward setting them apart from the dominant culture in which they lived. "They reserved the right to say where they had come from," I told my class. "They would not let anyone else do that for them, because they knew that their identity as a people depended on the stories they told about themselves."

The minute I said that, I knew the old woman was right. In her own stubborn way, she was refusing the dominant scientific culture's definition of her as the haphazard product of random variations. That creation myth was as unacceptable to her as the one about Marduk and Tiamat. She reserved the right to say where she had come from, and the Genesis story was the one she chose.

Evolutionary theory raises all kinds of interesting questions for science as well as for religion. In the first place, it seems to contradict the second law of thermodynamics—the law of entropy—which states that unless something is done to prevent it, all systems tend toward increasing disorder over time. The world we live in is full of examples. The roofs of abandoned houses collapse, mountains and shorelines erode, human beings age and die. But evolution works in the opposite direction, with more and more order evolving over time. Where does the requisite energy come from?

One of the most curious aspects of evolution is evidence from the fossil record that the process has not been a steady progression from simple to more complex organisms through random mutation and natural selection. Instead, there are long periods when few new forms emerge, followed by short periods in which new forms proliferate. At geological sites in the Grand Canyon and in the Pecos Wilderness above Santa Fe, it is possible to see a phenomenon called "The Great Unconformity," an apparent two-hundred-fifty-million-year gap in the fossil record. No one seems quite sure what to make of it. Does it mean that entire eras of life on earth left no remains at all? Does it mean that the remains somehow suffered erosion? Or does it mean that our geological time scale is off?[3]

We also know that animals evolve backwards, losing traits instead of acquiring them. Among human traits that have been lost or reduced over time are tails, body hair, wisdom teeth, the ability to synthesize vitamin C, the size of our teeth and appendix, the thickness of our skulls, and the bony ridges over our eyes. While we tend to take such losses for granted (and are grateful for a few of them), we may overlook the fact that these traits took many thousands or millions of years to evolve in the first place. Why would any organism slough off such hard-won features? What evolutionary force accounts for their loss?[4]

We also do not hear much about the other hominid species whom we beat out in the evolutionary foot race, including *Australopithecus afarensis* and

Homo neanderthalensis. While we are accustomed to thinking of ourselves as the only human species on earth, paleontologists are accumulating evidence that multiple human species are the norm instead of the exception. At almost any moment in prehistory, our family tree included several species of erect, upright walking primates. The fact that we have had no human cousins since the Neanderthals vanished some thirty thousand years ago is "an evolutionary aberration."[5]

For many people, the biggest question mark in evolutionary theory is not about how traits were selected but about how they were generated in the first place. Hugo DeVries, an early twentieth-century evolutionary scientist, said he was not interested in the *survival* of the fittest but in the *arrival* of the fittest.[6] Where did genes come from? How did life begin?

Because I have a mind like a layer cake, I have never felt compelled to choose between the story Genesis tells and the story Darwin tells. Separated by a layer of metaphoric possibility, they coexist peacefully enough for me, although I clearly believe there is a divine hand at work in the mix somewhere. In scientific terms this makes me a hypocrite, since the purposelessness of evolution is not optional but essential to the theory. At least I am in good company. In 1996, Pope John Paul II endorsed evolution as part of God's master plan, just four years after he lifted the Roman Catholic Church's three-hundred-fifty-year-old condemnation of Galileo. When he first ordered a reexamination of Galileo's case in 1980, he made a statement that might have applied to Darwin as well.

"Research performed in a truly scientific manner can never be in contrast with faith," he said, "because both profane and religious realities have their origin in the same God."[7]

If you read very much in evolutionary biology or cosmology, you are bound to encounter "the anthropic principle." Instead of trying to explain how the universe gave rise to life, the anthropic principle reverses the process, beginning with life and working backward to deduce the initial conditions required for its appearance. In its "weak form," the principle states that since we are here, the universe must have been put together in a certain way. In its "strong form," it says that the universe was bound to produce us, since our consciousness makes it possible for the world to exist. An old Jewish folk tale makes the same point. One day God said to Abraham, "If it weren't for me, you wouldn't be here," to which Abraham replied, "True, but if I weren't here there wouldn't be anyone to think about you."[8] In either of its forms, the anthropic principle recognizes that we live in a finely-tuned universe, and that without that fine-tuning there would be no intelligent life.

Sir Fred Hoyle's name comes up a lot in explanations of the anthropic principle. His research into carbon atoms explored the question of why there is such an abundance of carbon in our galaxy when its creation requires a triple collision of helium nuclei, which is quite rare. The answer lay in the internal resonances of carbon and oxygen nuclei, where figures as small as half a percent make all the difference between carbon and no carbon. Since carbon is essential for life, that half a percent also makes all the difference between us and no us.

Hoyle said that his atheism was shaken by this discovery. "A common sense interpretation of the facts," he wrote, "suggests that a superintellect has monkeyed with physics, as well as with chemistry and biology, and that there are no blind forces worth speaking about in nature. The numbers one calculates from the facts seem to me so overwhelming as to put this conclusion almost beyond question."[9]

While many scientists would beg to differ (they hold to the "cosmological principle," which says that human existence is incidental to the wider world), the philosopher and mathematician Bertrand Russell has perhaps offered the best criticism of the anthropic principle. "The believers in Cosmic Purpose make much of our supposed intelligence but their writings make one doubt it," he wrote. "If I were granted omnipotence, and millions of years to experiment in, I should not think Man much to boast of as the final result of all my efforts."[10] Even after you take his remark with the requisite grain of salt, Russell raises a very interesting question. *Is* humankind the final result of evolution? *Have* we gone as far as we can go, or is there more to hope for?

In his book *Servanthood: Leadership for the Third Millennium,* Bennett Sims speaks of Jesus as the prototype of an entirely new level of evolving humanity. As much as Jesus may have looked like any other *homo sapiens* (cunning humanity), Sims says, he was not. He was the firstborn *hetero pacificus* (peaceable humanity), who came to bring a new species of creature into being.[11] Of course this is theology and not biology, but it may rescue us from any illusion we have that we constitute the crowning achievement of creation. As long as we go on poisoning the planet of our birth and slaughtering one another in record numbers, our successful adaptation to our environment seems far from finished.

Meanwhile, scientists tell us that biological evolution may truly have come to an end. With the development of symbolic thought some forty thousand years ago, *homo sapiens* won an edge over their Neanderthal cousins, who left no evidence of any rituals, language, or belief in an afterlife. All these years later, our ability to use our brains innovatively has resulted in mind-boggling technology that essentially eliminates natural selection. In large parts of the world, weak and strong alike have access to food, medicine, and shelter. Residents of Atlanta's city housing projects are likely to have a longer life span than the medieval monarchs of Europe.

While we alter our physical environment with everything from nuclear fusion to auto emissions, genetic engineering will eventually allow us to change basic characteristics of our species to order. What would Darwin say? After millions of years, evolution by random selection—operating blindly and purposelessly, according to his theory—has produced a creature able to overturn the process.

My interest in these pages is not to argue for or against evolution or anything else. There is already a hot battle going on between classical evolutionary theorists and a group of anti-evolutionists who

defend something called "intelligent design theory."
While I am intrigued by many of the same holes in
evolutionary theory that interest this second group, I
do not share their dedication to discrediting Darwin.
I am much more interested in the questions science
and religion raise for one another, and in the eroding
boundary between the two. Even the old distinction
between science as the study of "how things work"
and religion as the study of "why" does not satisfy for
long. Who can really keep those two questions separate?

Darwin said that his blood ran cold every time he
looked into a vertebrate eye. Trying to imagine how
many lucky mutations had to occur in order to come
up with one eyeball taxed his faith in his own hypothesis, especially since eyes have apparently developed
not once but many times throughout the ages.
According to British biologist Brian Goodwin, "The
eye developed independently in more than forty lineages during evolution," which suggests to him that
natural selection is not the only force at work in the
evolving order of creation.[12]

Between Genesis and Darwin lies a third alterna-
tive few of us learned about in school: a creation
dependent neither on a literal reading of the Bible nor
on the random variations of genes but on laws of
complexity we are only beginning to understand. In
this story of creation, there is something beyond blind
chance at work in evolution. Instead of a collection of
genetic accidents, there are patterns more like blueprints that tend to organize cells the same basic way
every time. These patterns explain why something as

biologically complex as an eyeball can evolve in forty separate lineages.

Imagine stirring a bathtub full of water with your hand. You know more or less what you will create when you do that. The water is not going to shoot straight up toward the ceiling, nor is it going to remain motionless. The water has its own dynamic of self-organization, which rules out those two possibilities. When you stir the water, you are going to create some form of ripples and waves every time. Their size and shape may change, but the general pattern is predictable. In the same way, explains the science writer George Johnson, "Eyes are not random accumulations of accidents, but patterns that arise 'as waves and spirals arise naturally in water'."[13] Stir the water and you get waves. Stir the gene pool and you get eyes, kidneys, spinal cords and brains. Stir it again and the details may change, but the patterns will remain familiar, thanks to the dynamics of self-organization.

The biologists exploring this line of thought are sometimes called "structuralists," since they see complex structures at work in evolution. While no purely physical mechanisms can be found to explain these self-organizing structures, they are evident in everything from homeostasis to the patterns in flower petals and butterfly wings. What they suggest is that acceptance of evolution may not have to mean acceptance of a haphazard creation. It may also mean acceptance of a creation governed by certain biological designs. Where do those designs come from? That depends on whom you ask. Since religion is under no obligation to prove its answer, the answer seems easy. Designs come from a Designer, of course.

Since science proceeds by proof, it cannot say where complexity comes from, but it is hard not to be charmed by this idea: that in us, the design has evolved creatures who are capable of discerning the design. Like chickens penetrating the mysteries of their own eggs, we have been given the ability to glimpse our own origins. Imagine your own eyeball pressed against the eyepiece of a microscope, looking down at the kind of light-sensitive cell from which it evolved. Now imagine that light-sensitive cell squinting back at you. How many millions of years are spanned in that glance? Enough to make the most sophisticated mind spin.

I suppose it is predictable that a believer would like the structuralist view of things, since it leaves room for the divine mystery of design. It remains one story of creation among many, each with its own version of the truth. For people of faith, the story matters, but what matters even more is what we make of the story. What is the story behind the story? What is the meaning behind the so-called facts?

Forever and ever, one way Christians have spread the gospel is by learning the stories of the dominant cultures in which they live and then retelling them from a Christian perspective. That is how the pagan festival of the winter solstice in late December became the festival of Jesus' birth. We took a celebration of the s-u-n and turned it into a celebration of the s-o-n. That is also why Easter falls on the first Sunday on or after the first full moon on or after the spring equinox.

The date does not have anything to do with the exact day Jesus rose from the dead. We simply took over an ancient fertility festival of new life on earth and re-interpreted it as a sacred festival of new life in Christ.

Do you see how it works? There are facts and there is meaning, but the same facts do not necessarily produce the same meaning. What is to prevent us from reinterpreting the scientific creation story from a perspective of faith? It would not be science anymore, since science operates by empirically verifiable facts, but it might satisfy our need for a story that does not divide truth in half.

One reason I believe so many lay people are reading science right now is that it offers them a way to approach the mystery of the universe without all the dogma and divisiveness they have come to expect from religion. Science has its own dogma and divisiveness, of course, but so far as I know there has been no bloodshed over quantum mechanics or chaos theory. Several years ago the comparative mythologist Joseph Campbell won a great number of followers by illuminating the great mythical themes that emerge over and over again throughout the world's religions. Part of his appeal, I believe, was the glimmer of unity he offered to people who were weary to death of their divisions. While honoring the individual contributions of different traditions, he also affirmed their common ground in the stories they tell.

The American astrophysicist Brian Swimme makes an eloquent case for how badly humankind needs a new creation story right now. Having grown up on national stories, regional stories, ethnic stories, and religious stories, he says, we have been shaped by narratives that teach us to focus on our differences from one another. Many of those same stories also teach us to see ourselves as separate from the planet in whose bosom we are nested. Without diminishing the importance of those stories, Swimme calls for a "panhuman" story—a cosmic story—not tied to one cultural tradition or political ideology. A side benefit of such a story might be its focus on God, instead of humankind, at the center of the universe. But even without mentioning God by name, the scientific creation story makes pretty good reading.

Once upon a time, say fifteen billion years plus one day ago, neither "time" nor "space" had any meaning. There is not much more to say about that, except that nothing existed save a pinpoint of probability smaller than a proton that was the egg of the universe—what scientists call a "singularity." Then the egg exploded—who knows why—and the universe expanded a trillion trillion times, curving to such a degree that particles popped out of quantum nowhere.[14] When the universe was one second old, "every spoonful of stuff was denser than stone and hotter than the center of the sun."[15]

As it expanded, energy cooled into what we call matter, beginning with particles and antiparticles. As they routinely annihilated each other in explosions of light—the first war in heaven—it looked as if they would cancel each other out. But that is not what happened. Because the fundamental processes of producing matter contain an infinitesimal asymmetry (101 million particles of matter for every 100 million particles of antimatter), matter won out by the narrowest of margins and expansion continued. As the temperature dropped, hydrogen and helium formed in the few moments they could. Then the temperature dropped some more so that heavier elements never had a chance to form.

38

All of this occurred in the first five minutes. After that, the universe settled into a half-million-year cooling cycle during which little else happened. The cosmos existed as a hot cloud of ionized hydrogen and helium. Then the temperature dropped some more and stars began to form under the influence of gravity. As they grew in mass, things heated up inside of them, turning them into nature's own nuclear fusion reactors. Using hydrogen as fuel, they converted the lighter elements into heavier ones such as carbon and iron. Eventually the new stars became middle-aged stars and finally old stars whose nuclear reactors broke down. Unable to defend themselves against their own gravity, the stars collapsed in on themselves, creating so much heat inside of them that they exploded in supernova. These were spectacular funerals. A supernova can release more energy in one minute than all the other stars in the sky combined. As it does, it bequeaths all its elements to the galaxy, seeding the cosmos with oxygen, carbon, hydrogen, and nitrogen.[16]

If you remember your organic chemistry, then you know that these are the four elements most necessary for life. Our bodies are 65 percent oxygen, 18 percent carbon, 10 percent hydrogen, and 3.3 percent nitrogen, plus a smattering of the elements you can find listed on the bottle of your multi-mineral pills. Where did all those elements come from? From the creation of the cosmos. From the ashes of stars. Chemically speaking, the only difference between us and trees or rocks or chickens is the way in which our elements are arranged. During World War I, when blood was in short supply, wounded soldiers were sometimes transfused with sea water—and it worked! We are all made out of the same stuff. We are all children of the universe.[17]

Since you surely recognize this story as the story of the big bang, I should remind you that it is only a theory. A rival theory proposes that the universe is endlessly circulating into black holes and out of quasars, instead of expanding from a singularity at some finite point in history.[18] Technically, there are no true theories of the origins of the universe, since— as any scientist will tell you—a theory is an hypothesis that has been repeatedly tested over time. That will never happen with the universe, but cosmologists are busy working their way backward as fast as they can.

Back when the big bang model was first conceived early in the twentieth century, what scientists really needed was some evidence of cosmic background radiation. If the universe had begun with as big a bang as they thought, then some heat from that explosion should still exist. This notion occurred independently to at least three working groups of physicists, including Robert Dicke and James Peebles in Princeton, New Jersey. In 1964, while Dicke and Peebles were busy building a microwave horn that might allow them to detect the radiation, two astronomers named Arno Penzias and Robert Wilson at Bell Laboratories in Holmdel, New Jersey, were having trouble with their own antenna.

No matter where they pointed it, it picked up an irritating static they could neither get rid of nor explain. When they found pigeons nesting inside the antenna they thought they had found their problem. After evicting the birds and scraping up a substantial layer of their droppings, the astronomers taped the joints of the antenna and got back to work, but the noise was still there. It was there during the day, at night, in winter and summer, whether they aimed the antenna at the earth or at the Milky Way. When Penzias complained about the sound to a colleague who knew what Dicke and Peebles were doing at Princeton, everyone began to put two and two together.

Penzias called Dicke. Dicke drove to Holmdel. The two teams got together and realized that what they were hearing was nothing less than the hiss of fossil radiation still echoing from the big bang. Furthermore, the temperature of the sound was 2.7 degrees, which was the same value predicted a decade earlier by George Ganow and his colleagues Ralph Alpher and Robert Herman. Penzias and Wilson won a Nobel Prize for their discovery of cosmic background radiation, which effectively launched the science of cosmology.[19]

In 1992, when scientists found cosmic ripples in that background radiation that matched up with their best guesses about how galaxies came to be, Berkeley astronomer George Smoot told reporters that it was "like looking at the face of God."[20]

But how did all that "out there" result in what we think of as the us right here? You have no doubt heard what a close call it was. After the universe had been cooking along for ten billion years or so, our solar system congealed out of a nebular cloud. Earth did not start out blue and green, as we know it now. For those colors it needed life, and for life it needed water and organic molecules, both of which were delivered to earth by comets. The oldest rocks on the surface of the earth date back some 3.8 billion years.[21] A few of those rocks, off the coast of Australia, contain fossils of blue-green algae that are 3.5 billion years old.[22] The leap from those rocks to that algae is what no one, so far as I know, can explain.

What we do know is that the sun was exactly the right distance away for photosynthesis to occur, and that because it did occur, the oxygen in the atmosphere was maintained at 20.9 percent so that further life forms could emerge.[23] In the classical scheme, marine invertebrates were next, then more sophisticated plants, then fish with bones, then amphibians, then reptiles, then mammals, then birds, then primates, then us. I cannot recite this list without remembering a friend of mine, who came back from a therapeutic weekend in the seventies with scabs on her elbows and knees.

"What happened to you?" I asked her.

"We reexperienced our evolution," she said. "First we swam on our bellies like fish, then we crawled out of the slime, then we hopped on all fours."

Whatever the leader of the weekend had in mind, she was onto something. In the same way that the elements inside us link us to the stars, so our metabolisms link us to every other living creature. Every cell on earth, whether it belongs to a patch of blue-green algae or a human brain, consists of the same fifty organic molecules. Humans get their fuel from sugar while algae get theirs from the sun, but the basic reactions are the same. We all use four kinds of nucleotides. We all need twenty amino acids. We all carry our blueprints inside of us in the form of DNA or RNA.[24] The cells in our bodies are living fossils over 3.5 billion years old. What they suggest is that all life comes from the same source, which makes us all kin: algae, tadpoles, skunks, and blue jays, not to mention elephants and cats.

Depending on your point of view, I suppose you could read this as good news (all creation is related) or as bad news (who wants to be kin to a skunk?). As I said earlier, the facts themselves do not supply the meaning. An interpreter supplies the meaning—a sentient being who can perceive, wonder, think, and say.

When I survey this fifteen-billion-year-old history (which has more good guesses in it than hard facts), it is difficult to miss the most stunning miracle of creation: that in us, the universe has become conscious. We are the first creatures to articulate the motion of the planets. We are the first creatures to discern the commonality of all life. For those of us who believe God is the source from which we all arose, we are the first creatures to say so out loud.

This urge we have to understand the universe transcends the evolutionary model. This cosmic consciousness of ours is not necessary for our survival. We could eat, sleep, multiply, and prosper without ever thinking twice about where we came from or what it is all about.

Meanwhile, science cannot explain how human consciousness works or where it comes from. It is as much a mystery as the moment before the universe began. I spoke earlier of how much time is required for an eyeball to look back at a light sensitive cell. How much more time does it take for quantum particles to mature to the point where they may compose hymns of praise? Whether your answer is seven days or fifteen billion years, it remains a miracle that we are here at all, and able to praise our maker. God may well prefer the sound of spring peepers, but I have to believe there was joy in heaven when the first human being looked at the sky and said, "Thank you for this."

This is hardly original thinking on my part. Teilhard de Chardin, Loren Eiseley, Thomas Berry, and Sallie McFague have all written eloquently about the divine dimension of creation. But so has the British biochemist Arthur Peacocke, who wrote that "we are that part of the cosmos consciously capable of being aware of and of responding to that immanent Presence."[25]

Suddenly Paul's letter to the Romans sounds different to my ears. "For the creation waits with eager longing for the revealing of the children of God," he writes in the eighth chapter. Why should the creation look forward to creatures such as us? Because for all our manifold liabilities, we can still praise God. In human beings, matter has become aware of itself. In us, God has given all creation a voice.

While I was putting all this together, I asked a friend how I could relate it to the biblical story of creation. "Basically," I said, "it looks as if we all started out as rocks. The story I want to tell is how God taught the children of rocks to sing hymns, but how does that square with the book of Genesis?"

"Dust?" he said.

Of course! Dust. Why didn't I think of that? Dust is all God has ever needed to make life: the quantum dust from which the stars arose, the stardust by which the primal elements were sown, the earth dust from which the rocks were made, and the rock dust on which the first creatures grew.

"Then the LORD God formed man from the dust of the ground, and breathed into his nostrils the breath of life; and the man became a living being" (Genesis 2.7). Whichever version of the story you choose to believe, here is ample reason to rejoice.

III

The Physics of Communion

I celebrate myself, and sing myself,
And what I assume you shall assume,
For every atom belonging to me
*   as good belongs to you.*

WALT WHITMAN

B efore anyone enters the strange universe of quantum physics, it is necessary to recognize "the word problem." Since this largely unseen world defies common sense and refuses to behave like the visible world in which we hit tennis balls and drive cars, our usual ways of describing reality leave a great deal to be desired. The language of physics is math, not English, and those who cannot do the math should be wary of thinking they understand quantum mechanics. "Language evolved to help people get around on earth," writes George Johnson, "not down inside atoms."[1]

No one has ever seen a quark, for instance. These particles within particles were invented by Murray Gell-Mann in 1961 because he needed them to make one of his theories work. The word itself alludes to a line from James Joyce ("Three quarks for Muster Mark") in *Finnegan's Wake*.[2] According to Gell-Mann, quarks exhibit such things as "flavor" and "color." There are "up" and "down" quarks. There were once "truth" and "beauty" quarks as well, but according to my friend Louis Jensen "this was a little much for the physics community, so they changed 'beauty' and 'truth' to 'bottom' and 'up'." But a quark remains a theoretical construct, leading Niels Bohr to say that "we must be clear, when it comes to atoms, language can be used only as in poetry."[3]

48
    Bohr's point is that our language is not adequate to describe things we cannot see, much less understand. The best we can do is to create images that give us some handle on how those things act. Thus physics is less concerned with what nature *is* than with what can be *said* about nature.

Bohr might as well have been talking about religion. (Once, when the astronomer Allan Sandage was overheard talking in a restaurant, he was mistaken for a minister.[4]) As a preacher, I spend most of my life pressed up against the limits of language. I do not have the foggiest idea who God really is. I am not even sure I want to know, since any such knowledge would by definition blow all my existing circuits. Still, it is my business to say what I can, so I too seek images for what can never be said, using words such as "up," "down," "beauty," and "truth." I remain clear, as Bohr said, that when it comes to God, language can be used only as in poetry.

Meanwhile, science has made some curious word choices of its own. Although Einstein is best known for his two theories of relativity, neither of them asserts relativity in any ordinary sense. In his special theory of relativity, Einstein declared that central aspects of nature are anything *but* relative. Natural laws remain constant regardless of motion, and the speed of light is an absolute for all observers whatever their frame of reference. In his general theory of relativity, Einstein described the way gravity molds space-time. "Einstein could have called his accomplishments the Special Theory of a Cosmic Absolute and the General Theory of Gravitational Absolute," writes Gregg Easterbrook. "How might twentieth-century thought have developed," he goes on to ask, "if its preeminent scientific mind had chosen to favor the word "absolute" instead of "relativity"?[5]

Likewise, chaos theory does not offer scientific proof of utter chaos in the cosmos. On the contrary, it describes laws of complexity that actually place boundaries on chaos. Meanwhile, word choices such as "relativity" and "chaos" support public perception that science has overthrown meaning. And since meaning is the domain of religion, this raises the question of competing worldviews, which is very much an issue in the dialogue between science and religion.

We human beings tend to base our worldviews on the prevailing physics of the day. While I have heard the argument made the other way around, it seems true to me that our governments, our schools, our economies, and our churches all reflect our understanding of how the world works, and when that understanding changes—as it is changing right now—all of those institutions are up for revision. If you are familiar with Margaret Wheatley's work, then you know that her insights into the new science have changed the way some organizations are being managed in this country. If you are an educator, then you know that new theories about how the mind works have changed the way you do your job. As someone invested in the body of Christ, I am vitally interested in what changes may be up for the church as well.

While the Bible has no overt interest in cosmology apart from God's sovereignty over it, the basic concept seems to be that of a three-tiered universe, with a flat earth supported by pillars below and capped by the round dome of the heavens above. The waters above the heavens explained why the sky is blue, and the waters below the earth went down into the abyss. As early as five hundred years before Christ, the Greeks had figured out that this could not be so. If the earth were flat, then why did it cast a round shadow on the moon during a lunar eclipse? Eudoxus of Cnidos was the first to put forward a planetary theory based entirely on spherical motions.[6] Aristotle's adoption of it, with a round earth sitting at the center of the universe, made it the cosmology to be reckoned with for some two thousand years.

While Rome was too busy conquering the world to care very much what was going on in the sky, Christianity was focused on the world after this one. As Saint Ambrose put it in the fourth century, "To discuss the nature and position of the earth does not help us in our hope of the life to come." A little before him, Tertullian had sighed, "For us, curiosity is no longer necessary."[7] Before they could say, "Wait! We take it back!" their words had become prophetic. The Dark Ages descended on Europe and science guttered out like a lamp deprived of oil.

While scholars such as Thomas Aquinas continued to think in the dark, it was almost a thousand years before there was a renaissance of learning in Europe. With the invention of the printing press, intellectual classics that had lain dormant for centuries suddenly became both available and affordable. A Pole named Mikolai Kopernik could not get enough of them. He read his way from Cracow to Bologna and back again, returning home with volumes of Aristotle, Euclid, Archimedes, and Ptolemy in his luggage. He also came home with the name most of us know him by — Copernicus — the man who changed our vision of the universe.

Through his observation of the seasons and his reading of the classics, Copernicus believed that the sun, not the earth, belonged at the center of things. He also guessed what trouble that swap might cause, which was why he delayed publication of his work until his death was imminent. Although the church was undergoing its own revolution at the time, both Protestants and Catholics agreed on Copernicus. "Who will venture to place the authority of Copernicus above that of the Holy Spirit?" John Calvin howled out loud, while Martin Luther simply called the man a fool.[8]

Some fifty years later, when Galilei Galileo surveyed the heavens through the telescope he had made, he concluded that Copernicus had been right. After a high-handed campaign to convert the pope to his cosmology, Galileo was ordered to appear before the Inquisition, where he was reminded that the issue was not scientific merit but obedience. In his defense,

Galileo quoted the words of Cardinal Baronio, who said, "The Bible tells us how to go to heaven, not how the heavens go."[9]

His inquisitors were not impressed. On June 22, 1633, when he was seventy years old, Galileo got down on his knees in the great hall of a Dominican convent in Rome and read the renunciation they had written for him.

> Wishing to remove from the minds of your Eminences and of every true Christian this vehement suspicion justly cast upon me, with sincere heart and unfeigned faith I do abjure, damn, and detest the said errors and heresies, and generally each and every other error, heresy, and sect contrary to the Holy Church; and I do swear for the future that I shall never again speak or assert, orally or in writing, such things as might bring me under similar suspicion.[10]

Galileo spent the last eight years of his life under house arrest in his villa outside Florence. While his daughter read him the seven daily psalms of penitence that were part of his sentence, the old man sat by the window, where he could watch the planets through his telescope.

In 1611, the King James translation of the Bible was published with a note to readers that creation had occurred on the evening before the twenty-third of October in the year 4004 BCE. In 1616, the Catholic church banned all books that suggested the earth moved at all. But the scientific revolution could not be stopped. It gathered momentum through the seventeenth century, fired by the work of a British mathematician and natural philosopher named Isaac Newton.

With the publication of his book *Principia,* which was published in 1687, Newton planted the seeds of a new worldview. In it, he laid down the laws of celestial dynamics. Reducing them to four simple algebraic formulas, he revealed a solar system that worked like a vast machine. The machine, he said, was made of parts—some of them as small as an atom and others as huge as the sun—but they all obeyed the same laws. In this way, he not only vindicated Galileo but also unseated Aristotle, who had believed that the heavens and the earth were governed by different laws.

Apparently Newton never meant to unseat God too. At the end of his book he wrote that "this most beautiful system of the sun, planets, and comets could only proceed from the counsel and dominion of an intelligent and powerful Being."[11] He could not explain where the laws came from unless they came from God, in other words, but the laws themselves left very little for a deity to do. God may have designed the machine and thumped it into motion, but once the thing got moving it seemed to do just fine all by itself. As far as the universe was concerned, God's job was most like that of a night watchman: someone who dozed in a lawn chair while the stars spun in their courses overhead.

On the whole, human beings were so charmed by the illusion of control Newton's metaphor offered that we began to see ourselves as machines too. Believing that Newton told us the truth about how the world works, we modeled our nations, our economics, our families, and ourselves on atomistic principles. You are you and I am I. If each of us will do our parts, then the big machine should keep on humming. If a part breaks down, it can always be removed, cleaned, fixed, and replaced. There is no mystery to a machine, after all. According to Newton's instruction manual, it is perfectly predictable. If something stops working, any reasonably competent mechanic should be able to locate the defective part and set things right again.

While Christianity resisted this metaphor for a while, the illusion of control proved too hard to pass up. Theology became increasingly specialized and systematized. Our "God view" came to resemble our worldview. In many places, it is still possible to hear God described as a being who behaves almost as predictably as Newton's universe. Pull this lever and a reward will drop down. Do not touch that red button, however, or all hell will break loose. In this clockwork universe, the spiritual quest is reduced to learning the rules in order to minimize personal loss (avoid hell) and maximize personal gain (achieve salvation).

The emphasis on individual welfare is no mistake, either. It goes with the Newtonian world view, in which the atom is the basic building block of the cosmos. In the physical universe, even something as huge as the sun is made up of tiny atoms, which is why it behaves the same way they do. All big things can be broken down into small things, and it is those small things—those single units of indivisible matter—that count. No whole creation is more than the sum of its parts. To understand the whole, all you have to do is understand the parts.

When this model is transposed to the human universe, the individual human being becomes the atom—the single unit of social matter that is the basic building block for all social groupings. Once again, all big things can be broken down into small things. Nations, communities, churches, and families are all reducible to the individuals who make them up. If a child acts out, take the child to a counselor. Fix the child, without ever inquiring into the health of the family. If a poor woman sells crack to feed her children, send the woman to jail. Punish the woman, without ever asking about the society in which she lives.

In this clockwork universe, the way to keep the whole thing running is to focus on the parts. If one of them breaks down, then repair it. If it cannot be repaired, then replace it. There is nothing wrong with the whole that cannot be fixed by tinkering with the parts. There is no such thing as the whole. The individual is the fundamental unit of reality.

Recently I spent a couple of days at a Benedictine monastery in California. It was a gorgeous place, with a courtyard garden full of fragrant orange trees and a retreat house full of antiques. When I first came through the door, one of the brothers glided up to me and said, "I know what you're thinking: 'If this is poverty, I can't wait to see chastity!'"

Four times a day, a bell rang in the courtyard. As soon as it did, the brothers stopped whatever they were doing, put clean white robes on over their work clothes, and met in the chapel to pray. The rest of us were welcome to join them, but our presence was not required. If we did not show up then they would pray for us, as they prayed for everyone else in the world—for those who were present along with those who were absent, for those who were inclined toward God along with those who were not, for those who were in great need of prayer along with those who were not aware they needed anything at all.

Prayer was their job, and they took it seriously. They prayed like men who were shoveling coal into the basement furnace of some great edifice. They did not seem to care whether anyone upstairs knew who they were or what they were doing. Their job was to keep the fire going so that people stayed warm, and they poured all their energy into doing just that.

In their presence, I realized how atomistic many prayers are. So many of us pray chiefly as individuals. We confess our own sins, give thanks for our own blessings, ask God to address our own concerns. Even those with voluminous prayer lists can feel as if they are working alone, racing through the dark with their petitions like a midnight mail carrier.

Twentieth-century theology bears the marks of the Newtonian worldview, both in terms of its faith in reason and its urge to compartmentalize. Over the past hundred years or so, the study of theology has been divided up into parts that require prefixes: biblical, historical, systematic, practical, feminist, wom-

anist, liberation, and so forth. Similarly, most seminary curricula are divided into four separate areas of
study with courses taught by professors who are
rarely caught in each other's classrooms. While everyone agrees how important it is for students to synthesize all this learning, they may have a hard time
finding anyone on campus who can show them by
example how this is done. While most parish minis-
ters still function as general practitioners, they receive
the lion's share of their training from theological
specialists.

In most places, clinical pastoral education is part
of that training. Seminary students are packed off to
hospitals, community mental health centers, or resi-
dential treatment programs where they learn the
basics of Freudian theory along with certain helpful
psychotherapeutic techniques. Later, when they put
this knowledge to use in their churches, they will find
that it works well enough with individual parish-
ioners but offers little insight into the complex life of
communities. Why? Because Freud's worldview was
that of Newton and Descartes, in which individual
parts bump up against each other, project their mental stuff all over each other, and react.

Perhaps this is why so many large churches
resemble corporations, complete with departments,
ranked staff members, and organizational charts.
Even in churches with congregational polities, the
pictures tend to look like pyramids, with straight
lines of power that run from top to bottom. At one
parish I served, I was determined to discover an alter-

native and finally came up with a chart that looked more like a zinnia.

At the center of five concentric circles was the Holy Spirit. Emanating from that was a circle for the lay and ordained leaders of the church, with tendrils that reached into the next circle, where all the functioning committees of the church were found. That circle in turn reached into the larger circle of the entire membership of the church, and that circle opened onto the world beyond the church.

The first time I put that chart on the table with my lay leaders, I might as well have lit some incense and begun the meeting with a round of chanting "OM." The corporate types were appalled. They wanted lines of authority, not spheres of influence. They wanted to know who was responsible for what and where the buck stopped. Where was the top of this thing, anyway? What do you mean there is not a top, only a center? And why all the porousness between one circle and the next? Why can't the finance committee just do its job without revisiting the mission of the church? Isn't that the mission committee's job?

I could not blame them. I like straight lines myself, especially when my goal is getting from point A to point B. The problem was that I never could eke one single straight line out of parish ministry. For years, I would pull out my compass in the morning, plot a straight course to my goal for the day and find myself six miles off the path by noon. It was all those *people* who fouled things up. Over and over again, they would show up without appointments to talk about their unhappiness with the church cleaning woman, or a new idea they had for Sunday school, or their fear of losing their middle daughter to drugs. Never once did any of them ask to see the church organizational chart first, to be sure I was the right person to talk to about these things.

Parish life was just as fluid at the community level. I learned never to predict the outcome of any meeting. The ones I thought would produce mushroom clouds often turned out to be wildly creative, while the ones I expected to be uneventful lasted the longest of all. There was simply no telling what would happen, especially when people listened to each other. One person would say something and the whole atmosphere in the room would change. A decision that had seemed inevitable was suddenly open to question. I often wished there were some way to track what happened in a room when individuals started acting as a community. The very air would become lighter. People would say eloquent things that surprised even them, leading other people to change the positions they had been devoted to one moment before.

Eventually I got the message that parish ministry was not and would never be about getting from point A to point B for me. It was not a journey with a beginning and an end. It was more like a dance, with a lot of wide open space to be explored. To spend my time trying to arrive at a particular point on the dance floor would have been to waste the music.[12] A much more promising prospect was to learn how my different partners moved, and to swap as many dance steps with them as I could.

In other words, there is another way to conceive of our life together. There is another way to conceive of our life in God, too, but it requires a different world-view — not a clockwork universe in which individuals function as discrete springs and gears, but one that looks more like a luminous web, in which the whole is far more than the parts.

In this universe, there is no such thing as an individual apart from his or her relationships. Every interaction — between people and people, between people and things, between things and things — changes the face of history. Reality is not a well-oiled machine that behaves in logical, predetermined ways. Instead, it is an ever-unfolding process that defies precise prediction. In it, order and chaos are not enemies but fraternal twins. Creation depends on both of them. Together they shape life.

If this sounds like religious language, it is not. It is language inspired by quantum physics, which has caused a revolution in the way we see our world. There is nothing wrong with Newton's old model, as far as it goes. The problem is that Newton believed the atom was indivisible — that it was the smallest possible particle in existence. Now we know there are even tinier bits of matter at the sub-atomic level, which do not operate the way Newton said they should. While his rules still work in the world we can see, there is another, very different set of rules at work in the world that *makes up* the world we can see.

My own introduction to the new science came five years ago, when I attended a clergy leadership conference at which Fred Burnham spoke. An Episcopal

priest with a doctorate in the history of science from
Johns Hopkins, Burnham is dedicated to holding
peace talks between science and religion. As a believer in one God, he cannot keep scientific truth and
religious truth in separate boxes. He was there to talk
to us about chaos theory, and in particular about how
the science of complexity might be useful to us as
parish leaders. While I had read some classical
physics and math before that, no one had ever suggested that it had anything to do with my life in the
church.

When I entered the room, Burnham was pecking
at the keyboard of a computer. The machine sat in
front of the blackboard on a low desk. The screen
remained blank as the group assembled. Then
Burnham greeted us, pressed "Enter," and turned his
back on the computer screen as he delivered his lecture. At the beginning there was nothing but one thin
green line snaking its way around the interior of the
screen. First it made something that looked like a lop-
sided figure eight and then it doubled back on itself —
roughly, not exactly — as if a young child had tried to
trace the design twice.

Burnham was apparently oblivious to what was
going on behind him. From time to time, so was I. I
did not know one thing about chaos theory. I had
always assumed I was incapable of understanding it,
but as Burnham introduced us to fractals, complexity,
and non-linear equations I had what I can only call a
religious experience. Jumping from the science to the
meaning I made of it, I understood why my life
would not run along straight lines. I understood why

my ten-year plans never work. And rather than feeling miserable about those things, I began to glimpse a deeper level of physical reality at which my life was behaving exactly as it should.

62

By calling this a religious experience, what I mean is that I experienced salvation in it. I was rescued from my atomistic understanding of myself in ministry, in which I was the mechanic and my parish the machine I was supposed to run. The new science gave me new metaphors for my life in community, which had far more chaos in it than Stephen Covey would deem acceptable but which was also embraced by a boundary I can only call love.

If I had been a better student of the Bible, none of this should have been news to me. But I am also a student of the culture, which is still hooked on the mechanical model of reality. In Burnham's classroom, I discovered another worldview that dissolved that dotted line down the middle of me. Both my reason and my faith were challenged by what I was seeing in front of me. Science seemed to be speaking to my spirit. As I watched the image on the computer screen develop into a design shaped like a butterfly, I thought, "This is *math*. No one ever told me math could be beautiful." When Burnham finally named the design—a "strange attractor"—and explained that it was a visual representation of the mathematical "magnet" that pulled randomness into some semblance of order, I knew I had found a window on the universe that would occupy me for some time to come.

If you have ever seen the design a free-swinging pendulum traces in sand, then you have seen an attractor at work. Since I am not a scientist, I am not always sure what I am looking at, nor do I have the theoretical background to discern all the implications of a particular phenomenon. But as a preacher (which is to say a roving reporter of life on the planet) I reserve the right to make meaning out of what I see. This drives some of my scientific friends crazy. They try to help me understand that science is not in the business of making meaning, and that the minute I wring metaphors out of scientific phenomena I have left the realm of fact for fiction. One critic has even warned me that as a nonscientist reading science I am in great peril: "Anyone who does not enter the sheepfold by the gate but climbs in by another way can be in a lot of trouble." I know it is so, but that knowledge does not seem to help me apply the brakes. As a believer in one God, I think everything is connected to everything else. What is exciting to me is that believers in science are beginning to think the same thing — not the God part but the connection part.

Early in the twentieth century, at the Institute for Advanced Study in Princeton, Albert Einstein and his colleagues Boris Podolsky and Nathan Rosen tried to undermine quantum theory with something now known as the EPR experiment (for *Einstein, Podolsky,* and *Rosen*). According to quantum theory, a subatomic particle that decays into two particles becomes a set of "twins" — a single system with two parts, spinning in opposite directions. No one knows which one is spinning "up" and which one is spinning "down" until a measurement is made, but according to the laws of physics they must always balance each other.

So far so good. Now imagine those two particles flying apart—one of them heading around the dark side of the moon while the other lingers in the laboratory above the nimbus of Einstein's hair. If Einstein could nab that one and reverse its spin, he theorized, then the other particle would have to reverse itself too—even if it were light years away. According to the laws of quantum physics, this is exactly what would happen. Because the two particles were in a state of "quantum entanglement" (Erwin Schrodinger's phrase[13]) they would behave in complementary ways no matter how far apart they were. Since this eerie idea violated Einstein's own theory of special relativity—he called it "spooky action at a distance"—he concluded that quantum theory was wrong.[14]

Unhappily for him, subsequent experiments proved him wrong instead. Once two particles have interacted with each other, they remain related regardless of their physical distance from one another. In some sense, they stay in contact through space and time, although the point does not seem to be that they are using some kind of faster-than-light communication. The much more confounding point seems to be that they do not behave as two separate particles, but one.

In scientific language, they must be considered a single non-separable object. Researchers think it has something to do with field theory—fields being invisible, non-material structures that may turn out to be the basic substance of the universe. You know about gravitational fields and electromagnetic fields. If you stand under a high power wire and hold a fluorescent light bulb in the air, there is a good chance it will light up, because you are standing in a power field. Well, imagine another kind of field that knits the whole cosmos together, so that a shiver in the Milky Way gives us a shiver right here, faster than the speed of light.

The science stops there, but my imagination goes on. I think about the mother who sits bolt upright in her bed in the middle of the night, "knowing" something has happened to her child. I think about the strange communication between twins, who may end up making similar choices in their lives even though they have been separated from birth. The meaning I make out of the EPR paradox is that such phenomena occur because the two are not really two but one. Each one "knows" what the other is doing not because they happen to be psychic but because they belong to the unbroken wholeness of the universe.

Consider Paul's metaphor of the church as Christ's body. As different as we are and as many functions as we serve, we are far more than a collection of parts. We may act that way sometimes, with the left side pulling against the right and the feet refusing to take a step until the hands have apologized, but there are also times when we clearly participate in some form of community—or better yet, communion—that translates us into the mind of Christ. The more in tune we are, the better we respond. This is not something that only happens to us person by person but something that happens to all of us at once. There is no explanation for it in terms of cause and effect. This head of ours, this guiding mind, does not speak into a tape recorder or send directions by fax, but plenty of us have experienced the presence as real.

In quantum physics, such mysterious action-at-a-distance is known as nonlocality, but it is only one of the phenomena that have changed the scientific landscape. Another is Heisenberg's uncertainty principle, which asserts that it is not possible to know both where a particle is and where it is going. The closer you come to determining its location, the further you go from determining its momentum. If you change your tactics and focus on its momentum, you will no longer be able to say where it is. In between your measurements, it exists as probability wave—a combination of all the possible ways it could go—which all remain possible until you focus on it. When you take your measurement, the wave collapses. It assumes an actual value, but only because you asked it to.

One analogy might be the strobe light under which some of us danced in the sixties. We were in constant motion in the darkness—hands in the air, heads thrown back—some of us with our eyes closed and others searching the crowd for a friend. It was a tableau that changed every second, with infinite possibilities. When the strobe came on, the probability wave collapsed. The light took our measure and we were captured in time, like a moving picture frozen on a single frame. An observer looking at that frame might say, "There is a woman who dances without moving her feet," to which the woman might say, "No, that is just how you happened to catch me at the moment. Take the measurement again and the picture will be different."

With quantum theory, there are no dancers, only the pictures. In a tenet of the new science that tries the most philosophical mind, a thing cannot even be said to be one thing or another until someone interrupts it to find out what it is. Plus, the interruption itself has to be taken into account. The moment you set up a scientific experiment, you become one of the dancers. The light you shine on a particle so that you can see it carries its own momentum, which bumps into the particle and changes its heading. You cannot observe the phenomenon without entering into relationship with it, and the relationship changes the equation.

Some physicists object that Heisenberg's uncertainty principle is a theoretical result. It is possible mathematically but not experimentally, since an electron exists more as a "spread" than a distinct entity. Strictly speaking, this means that an electron lacks the basic hallmarks of existence. "From the quantum angle," Paul Davies explains, "an electron is not simply an electron. Shifting energy patterns shimmer around it, financing the unpredictable appearance of photons, protons, mesons, and even other electrons. In short, all the paraphernalia of the subatomic world latches on to an electron like an intangible, evanescent cloak, a shroud of ghostly bees swarming around the central hive."[15] That is what makes it generally impossible to measure. It is not a discrete individual, but part of a complex network of relationships.

If you are feeling a little disoriented right now, let me assure you that you are in very good company. The people who discovered all this stuff were a little dazed by it too. Werner Heisenberg, the originator of the uncertainty principle, remembers late night discussions with Niels Bohr that ended almost in despair. Recalling one of them, Heisenberg wrote, "When at the end of the discussion I went alone for a walk in the neighboring park, I repeated to myself again and again the question: Can nature possibly be so absurd as it seemed to us in these atomic experiments?"[16]

Bohr himself said, "Anyone who is not shocked by quantum theory has not understood it." Erwin Schrodinger, a fellow physicist, was even more blunt than that. "I don't like it," he said, "and I'm sorry I ever had anything to do with it."[17]

The reasons for their dismay are manifold. In the first place, the physical world seems to obey two different sets of rules. At the macro level of trees and rocks, Newtonian mechanics work just fine. A tree can be said to have a definite position in space and time, and a rock dropped from a window will fall at a predictable rate to a predictable spot on the ground. Everything in this world happens for a reason and can be explained in terms of cause and effect.

At the micro level of quantum particles, however, these rules no longer apply. A photon may be said to be both particle and wave. If you know where an electron is you cannot, by definition, know where it is going. If you know where it is going, you cannot know where it is. Furthermore, you cannot know any of these things without interacting with them, which means that you will never know how they behave when you are not watching.

While quantum mechanics is set up so that it works at the macro level, using it on that large scale would be like measuring the distance between Chicago and New York with a six-inch ruler. Meanwhile, Newtonian mechanics is so unwieldy at the micro level that employing it there would be akin to doing brain surgery with a bulldozer.[18] For all practical purposes, each level requires its own set of rules. Those of us who live in the macro world may well wonder how the big, visible objects in our world can behave differently from the tiny, invisible stuff of which they are made—where two things may act as one, and one as two.

The new science requires a radical change in how we conceive the world. It is no longer possible to see it as a collection of autonomous parts, as Newton did, existing separately while interacting. The deeper revelation is one of undivided wholeness, in which the observer is not separable from what is observed. Or, in Heisenberg's words, "the common division of the world into subject and object, inner world and outer world, body and soul is no longer adequate."[19]

Is this physics or theology, science or religion? At the very least, it is poetry. As far back as the thirteenth century, the Sufi poet Jelaluddin Rumi wrote, "You think because you understand *one* you must also understand *two,* because one and one make two. But you must also understand *and.*"

For John Polkinghorne, who was a mathematical physicist at Cambridge before he became an Anglican priest, the "and" between science and religion is their common search for truth. In a slim volume called *Quarks, Chaos and Christianity,* he makes some startling connections between the discoveries of physics and the articles of faith. Our experience of light as both particle and wave may give us a way to express our experience of Jesus as both human and divine, he says. Ask a human-like question and you get a human-like answer. Ask a divine-like question and you get a divine-like answer. As different as they may be, both languages are necessary. The deep truth is not either but both.[20]

Likewise, says Polkinghorne, the simple act of boiling water gives us a parable of what scientists call a "phase change." At 100 degrees Centigrade a very small amount of water becomes a very large amount of steam as H_2O moves from the liquid regime to the gaseous one. While the liquid and the gas behave in different ways, they remain the same substance. The laws of nature have not changed; only their consequences have. When Polkinghorne considers the mystery of Christ's death and resurrection, what he sees is a phase change. Jesus was the first puff of steam in a new regime, which some of us call the kingdom of God. As a physicist, Polkinghorne knows that a new regime is accompanied by new phenomena. In Jesus' case, those phenomena include the boiling up of death into everlasting life.[21]

One of the most interesting and controversial theoretical physicists in print is David Bohm, who died in 1992. Working in the area of relativistic quantum field theory pioneered by Paul Dirac, Bohm caught a glimpse of reality in which the universe neither occupies space and time nor contains many different things. Rather, he said, it behaves more like one interwoven thing that takes time and space seriously but not too seriously — perhaps by treating them as idioms that the universe finds necessary in order to communicate itself to observers.[22]

While he said that as a scientist, I heard him as a theologian, and began to wonder if the universe might have a "memory" that pre-dates the big bang. Back before that explosion triggered the expansion of time and space, there was that egg of the universe in which all places were one place and all things were one thing. I would call it the garden of Eden, only the beauty of the garden lay in its diversity. The beauty of this earlier reality was its unity, its total coherence. Mind, matter, and time were not yet different. They were all floating in the same yolk. Then the universe was born and the one became many. Quantum particles became planets, galaxies, clusters, and superclusters. Atoms became blue-green algae, toads, palm trees, and swans. Space became here or there, as time became then or now.

But what if deep down in the being of these many things remains the memory of their being one, which makes them behave in ways which torture scientists? Space and time are not separable. Light is both particle and wave. A particle way over there responds instantly to a particle way over here, as if the two were not two but one.

What if our mental torture only comes about because we insist on conceiving reality as many when it is truly and deeply one? All appearances to the contrary, "the universe remains as it was in the beginning, when all places were one place, all times one time, and all things the same thing."[23] Explaining Bohm's work, Timothy Ferris suggests that "the universe began as a hyperdimensional bubble of space, all but four of the dimensions of which compacted to form what we today call subatomic particles. Those particles look to us like zillions of individual things, but that is merely their appearance in the four dimensions of spacetime. In hyperspace they could very well still be *one* thing—could, therefore, be not only connected but identical."[24]

Once, when the physicists John Wheeler and Richard Feynman were discussing string theory, Wheeler said, "Feynman, I know why all electrons have the same charge and the same mass."

"Why?" Feynman asked.

"Because they are all the same electron!" Wheeler replied.

The writer of Ephesians put it like this: "There is one body and one Spirit...one Lord, one faith, one baptism, one God and Father of all, who is above all and through all and in all" (4.4-6). We have made much of the "above all" in Christian theology, placing God at the top of the organizational chart of the universe and ourselves, as God's deputies, right below. But what about the "through all and in all" part of the equation? In a world like ours, which even the new science calls a web of relationship, there is no place to stand apart from and above the rest of creation. Only in the most abstract sense can we assert our sovereignty over blue-green algae, toads, palm trees, and swans. Our dominion, such as it is, lies in the privilege of our consciousness. We among all the others have been given the job of keeping covenant. We among all the others have been given the privilege of knowing whom to thank. Meanwhile, we live in covenant with every living creature of all flesh, and our survival depends on our responsiveness to that fact.

In Sunday school, I learned to think of God as a very old white-bearded man on a throne, who stood above creation and occasionally stirred it with a stick. When I am dreaming quantum dreams, what I see is an infinite web of relationship, flung across the vastness of space like a luminous net. It is made of energy, not thread. As I look, I can see light moving through it as a pulse moves through veins. What I see "out there" is no different from what I feel inside. There is a living hum that might be coming from my neurons but might just as well be coming from the furnace of the stars. When I look up at them there is a small commotion in my bones, as the ashes of dead stars that house my marrow rise up like metal filings toward the magnet of their living kin.

Where am I in this picture? I am all over the place. I am up there, down here, inside my skin and out. I am large compared to a virus and small compared to the sun, with a life that is permeable to them both. Am I alone? How could I ever be alone? I am part of a web that is pure relationship, with energy available to me that has been around since the universe was born.

Where is God in this picture? God is all over the place. God is up there, down here, inside my skin and out. God is the web, the energy, the space, the light — not captured in them, as if any of those concepts were more real than what unites them — but revealed in that singular, vast net of relationship that animates everything that is.

At this point in my thinking, it is not enough for me to proclaim that God is responsible for all this unity. Instead, I want to proclaim that God *is* the unity — the very energy, the very intelligence, the very elegance and passion that make it all go. This is the God who is not somewhere but everywhere, the God who may be prayed to in all directions at once. This is also the God beyond all directions, who will still be here (wherever "here" means) when the universe either dissipates into dust or swallows itself up again. Paul Tillich's name for this divine reality was "the ground of all being." The only thing I can think of that is better than that is the name God revealed to Moses: "I Am Who I Am."

This shift in my image of God is so radical that calling God "she" seems minor by comparison. It is not a matter of my sudden conversion to pantheism (of which I am often accused), since that belief system makes no provision for a God beyond creation. But I do plead guilty to pan*en*theism, which understands God to be both transcendent and immanent. As Joseph Campbell once asked, what if the universe is not merely the product of God but also the manifestation of God—a "eucharistic planet" on which we have been invited to live?

"I Am Who I Am" does not sound to me like the self-identification of a deity who stands over reality and sometimes stirs it with a stick. Instead, it sounds like the singular utterance of the only One who ever was, is, or shall be, in whom everything else abides. For the moment, we see through a glass darkly. We live in the illusion that we are all separate "I ams." When the fog finally clears, we shall know there is only One.

IV

The Limits of Knowledge

It is not sufficient any longer to listen at the end of a wire to the rustlings of galaxies; it is not enough even to examine the great coil of DNA in which is coded the very alphabet of life. These are our extended perceptions. But beyond lies the great darkness of the ultimate Dreamer, who dreamed the light and the galaxies. Before act was, or substance existed, imagination grew in the dark.

LOREN EISELEY

The physicist Niels Bohr, who was so conscious of the limits of language, liked to tell the story about the young rabbinical student who went to hear three lectures by a famous rabbi. Afterward he told his friends, "The first talk was brilliant, clear and simple. I understood every word. The second was even better, deep and subtle. I didn't understand much, but the rabbi understood all of it. The third was by far the finest, a great and unforgettable experience. I understood nothing and the rabbi didn't understand much either."[1]

Since I have studied under Rabbi Jesus, this story makes perfect sense to me. There are things no one can talk about. If we insist on trying, as we are inclined to do, then something unforgettable may happen in the air around our words, but it will not be because we understand them in any rational sort of way. The experience will be one of worship—or awe—which involves a different kind of understanding.

Recently a friend asked me what I had been reading lately. Thrilled to have an audience, I spun through some of the same discoveries I have shared with you: the structuralist version of evolutionary biology, the EPR paradox, and David Bohm's vision of quantum unity. When I finished, my friend said, "That's impressive, but what does it have to do with Jesus of Nazareth?"

One plausible answer is, "Nothing, absolutely nothing at all." Insofar as Jesus came to show us what true love meant, reconciling us to God and one another in the process, science has nothing to add. Trying to follow Jesus in the way of that love is as hard now as it ever was, and God alone has the power to help us do it. However much we may gain from a dialogue between scientific and religious knowledge, the latter is by far the more demanding of the two. I can believe in the big bang without losing one minute's sleep about how much stuff I own, and my acceptance of Heisenberg's uncertainty principle does not make any requirements of me in terms of how I treat you. Because science does not deal in ethics or morals, it cannot tell me how to live or whom to love. All it can tell me is how the world works—or how it may work—and then refer me elsewhere for answers about how to live honorably in such a world.

But there is another answer that makes sense to me, and it is that I believe in an incarnate God, which is to say, a God who has chosen to be revealed in physical form. In Hebrew scripture, the first form of that self-revelation was the universe itself. God spoke, and God's word became sun, moon, earth, stars, us. Later God spoke some more and God's word became Torah. In Christian scripture, God's self-revelation took the form of one particular human being. God spoke to a young girl in Nazareth and God's word became flesh. Jesus was born into the physical world, not to remain above it all but to live through it all and in it all, so that we might discover the holiness of our own lives in the flesh.

Because I believe all this, I take the physical universe very seriously. It matters to me because it mattered to Jesus and it matters to God. No part of it seems negligible to me. I read science for the same reason I read theology: because I am a seeker after truth. Meanwhile, both science and religion remind me that there are limits to my knowledge. No one knows what caused the big bang. No one knows the mind of God. When I encounter these limits—when the measly lasso of my reason falls a couple of million miles short of the living truth—then you would think I would be disappointed, but I am not. Instead, I am exhilarated. I experience a recovery of awe, which may be something else all this has to do with Jesus of Nazareth.

This leads me to say something about the difference between how religion and science "know" things. While both rely on reason and experience, the most obvious difference is that science depends on observation while religion depends on revelation. You "go get" the first kind of knowledge. The second kind is "given" to you.

In the scientific model, you watch something to see what you can find out about it. You plant twelve kernels of corn in little paper cups and track their germination. Presumably, what you collect from watching them are facts about their behavior that you may test to make sure they behave the same way every time. At the end of the process you have objective truth, which you can demonstrate to anyone who is interested.

In the religious model, truth is received by revelation. The revelation may come secondhand, as you read Bible stories or listen to sermons. It may also come hot from the source, as you experience conversion or sense God's presence in a particularly difficult time. Either way, it is rarely about the world you can see, which makes it hard to collect anything science would recognize as fact. Revelation is more often about the world of relationship, which is notorious for its subjectivity.

In Luke's gospel, the angel Gabriel pays two separate visits to Zechariah and his young cousin Mary. The purpose of both visits is to announce the miraculous birth of a bouncing baby boy. Zechariah's boy will be named John, Gabriel says, and Mary's will be called Jesus. Both Zechariah and Mary are astounded by this news. Both of them ask, "How can this be?" but only Zechariah is struck dumb for his impertinence. Exhibiting an archangelic double standard, Gabriel leaves Mary alone. He will not behave the same way twice, any more than God will.

So there is subjectivity in the revelation itself and more subjectivity in the interpretation of it. You and I may read the book of Daniel very differently. Even if we rise above our individual differences and appeal to the community of scholars, we will find that they too read Daniel very differently. This sort of thing has led to the assertion that religion deals with opinions, not facts.

Roughly put, scientific knowledge based on observation is credited with *objectivity, predictability* and *fact,* while religious knowledge based on revelation is assigned *subjectivity, unpredictability,* and *belief.* And yet as I have suggested in these pages, those distinctions no longer hold.

Cosmologists and evolutionary biologists freely admit that they cannot deal in absolute truth. Creation will not be repeated in our lifetimes. Science has valuable evolutionary models and exquisitely accurate cosmological models to offer us, but nothing that even qualifies as a theory, much less a fact. As long as a theory is defined as a hypothesis that has been repeatedly tested over time (as the theory of general relativity has), certain scientific ideas will remain in the realm of "belief."

As for objectivity, Heisenberg's uncertainty principle effectively put the quash on that. The moment you train a photon of light on an electron so that you can detect it, the photon will disrupt its motion. "To observe is to disturb,"[2] and no observation can be separated from the aims and methods of the observer. Science is full of subjectivity.

I will say more about predictability in a moment, but for now it is enough to point out that the best meteorologists in the world cannot predict precisely where a hurricane will hit the coastline. While they may be able to narrow the probabilities, they cannot foretell the future. They can only say what a hurricane has done when it is through.

What all of this means is that the distinction between scientific and religious knowledge is not as clear as it once was. Both are dedicated to the search for truth. Both are vulnerable to error. Both experience awe. One reason I am so drawn to the new science is its openness to the wonder of discovery. In my experience, organized religion is not always so open. Perhaps because its main job is to conserve and transmit a two-thousand-year-old tradition, the church seems more interested in protecting truth than in discovering it. New scholarship, new theology, new liturgy and new imagery are typically greeted with condescension if not outright hostility, as if God were more invested in what has already happened than in what happens next. If you doubt this, then simply refer to the Holy Spirit as "she" the next time you are in church and see what kind of reaction you get. When I am feeling positively stifled by religion's fear of the future and suspicion of change, a little dose of the new science does me a world of good.

Because science works with observable data and only "believes" things that can be repeated, it does not have the luxury of dogma. As much as Albert Einstein distrusted quantum theory and as hard as he worked to disprove it, the experiments themselves could not be denied. It turned out that there was more for him to learn, whether he liked it or not.

At this particular moment in time, what I am noticing is that some scientists have begun to speak of God while some theologians have begun to speak of proof. If you search the database at your local library, you may be able to find a book called *The Mind of God* by Australian theoretical physicist Paul Davies, or an article titled "Astronomical Evidences for a Personal, Transcendent God" by Canadian astrophysicist and Christian apologist Hugh Ross.

On the whole, crossovers such as these make pure scientists cringe. They point out that science is a method, not a body of knowledge. As long as God remains invisible and unpredictable, science has nothing to say on the subject. Furthermore, they point out, most of the people on the science-and-religion bandwagon are already believers. These people find the connections they are looking for, while non-believers examine the same evidence and find none. Carl Feit, a cancer biologist and Talmudic scholar, says, "I don't think that by studying science you will be forced to conclude that there must be a God. But if you have already found God, then you can say, from understanding science, 'Ah, I see what God has done in the world.'"[3]

The people most likely to be intrigued by the new dialogue between science and religion are those in the middle — people who want to believe in God but who have a hard time with all the requisite beliefs, especially those that seem to contradict natural law. While religion enjoins them to have faith, science expects them to ask questions.

Some religious thinkers make a distinction between belief, defined as intellectual assent to a particular set of theological convictions, and faith, defined as "an unreserved opening of the mind to the truth, whatever it may turn out to be."[4] Read from this perspective, the Bible is one long story about how

God demolishes human beliefs in order to clear space for faith. Ask Abraham and Sarah, ask Elijah and Paul. Ask anyone who was ever granted intimacy with God. The moment you think you have the formula worked out, God changes the equation. Just when you think Ishmael must be the child you have been waiting for, your wife takes your hand and presses it against her belly, where you feel the strong kick of a child named Isaac. Just when you think the voice of the Lord will fall like fire from heaven, it comes in the whispering sound of sheer silence. Just when you think you have the bad guys on the run, a bright light knocks you to the ground and says, "Saul, Saul, why do you persecute me?"

The Bible is full of stories about how our beliefs trip us up. So are our own lives. While most of us have acquired some useful maps for the journey (which include the teachings of both science and religion), very few of those maps are in mint condition. Instead, they have scribbles all over them: dotted lines for the shortcuts we have found, a circled area where blueberries grow all summer, a skull and crossbones over the well that has dried up. Our maps are always under revision. Whether the subject is science or religion, our beliefs are always challenged by our experience, which begs us never to put the lid on truth.

This is the definition of faith I want to go forward with: a radical openness to the truth, whatever it may turn out to be. While a scientist might blanch at the word, faith so defined is essential to science, and especially to the branch known as cosmology. Since the creation of the cosmos cannot be repeated (at least not in our lifetimes), how it began is anyone's best guess. According to one Native American creation myth, the earth rests on the back of a giant turtle. When an ethnologist who was trying to get the story down on paper asked an elder what was underneath that turtle, the elder said, "Another turtle."

"And under that?" the ethnologist asked.

"Oh, it's turtles all the way down."

Modern cosmologists offer a great deal more detail. By plugging in variables that describe how the universe is currently behaving, they can rewind the figures and come up with an educated guess about initial conditions. By observing that the universe is expanding, for instance, they can guess that there was an explosion at the beginning. But while there is broad consensus about the big bang model of the cosmos, it still has big holes in it. No one knows exactly how old the universe is, how big it is, or how quickly it is expanding. And no one can say who lit the fuse in the first place. However far back science is able to go, there is always the problem of a first cause. How does something come from nothing? How can there be a bang without a match?

Some of you learned this as one of the proofs for the existence of God, but whether your answer is "God," "quantum physics" or "it's turtles all the way down," some leap of faith is required. In order to say anything, you must begin by taking something for granted. You must adopt some point of view, and that is as true in science as in religion.

John Polkinghorne, who was a physicist before he was a priest, uses the example of a photograph from a bubble chamber. This chamber, which is a device for tracking the paths of elementary particles, is filled with almost boiling liquid. When particles pass through it, they trigger little chains of bubbles that make their paths visible. If you did not know this, then the photograph would make no sense to you. It would just look like an abstract drawing, with a few straight lines overlaid by some curly ones.

So Polkinghorne's first point is there are no uninterpreted facts. Without some knowledge of what a bubble chamber is and what it is for, you could not make heads or tails of the reality it reveals. Every picture of reality is taken from a certain perspective. "You can't just stare at the world," he says, "you have to view it from a chosen point of view."[5] His second point is that a particle physicist would know that some of the lines in the photograph are "strays"—tracks that have nothing to do with the experiment and must be ruled out before any conclusions are drawn.

The problem is that there is no one right way to do this. It is a matter of judgment—of informed opinion—which means that one scientist might rule out what another might leave in, leading them to two different interpretations of the same facts. Even in science, "there is no such thing as an immaculate perception."[6] Reading the results of an experiment calls for a combination of observation and inference. Some researchers who observe a phenomenon that defies known facts may dismiss it as an experimental error, while others scramble to come up with "auxiliary hypotheses."

The most shocking example of an auxiliary hypothesis, which few cosmologists will deny, is that we cannot make sense of how the universe works unless we posit that ninety-nine percent of it is invisible.[7] Everything we can see—all the millions of galaxies with their billions of stars—must account for no more than one percent of the cosmos. Otherwise there is no way to explain the orbits of the galaxies, which do not exhibit enough mass to spin as quickly as they do. Science's best guess is that these galaxies must be embedded in massive halos of dark matter—stuff that is undetectable because it neither emits nor absorbs light.

My advice is not to think about it too much, but the implications could be staggering. If the dark part of cosmic mass—which is the vast majority of it—turns out to behave differently from the light part, then there will be quite a lot of refiguring to do. According to science writer Timothy Ferris, scientific conclusions that ignore dark matter may be as distorted as "a poll that attempted to predict the outcome of a national election by interviewing only vegetarian monarchists."[8]

Meanwhile, all that dark matter is having a measurable effect on our own galaxy. The Milky Way galaxy—our home—belongs to a neighborhood of some twenty-six galaxies known as the Local Group. In the late 1980s, a team of astronomers called the Seven Samurai noted that the Local Group and thousands of nearby galaxies are sliding sideways at the speed of six hundred thirty kilometers per second, or about three times as fast as the sun's orbit around the center of the Milky Way. Relative to the universe as a whole, that is pretty fast.

90

The Seven Samurai believe the cause is a huge, invisible chunk of matter that lies two hundred million light years away, out past the Virgo and Hydra-Centaurus clusters. Those clusters are being yanked sideways too, even faster than we are. The hypothetical mass doing the yanking is called "The Great Attractor," for obvious reasons. Whatever else it is, it is huge — as big as fifty thousand galaxies — with ninety percent of it dark matter.[9]

That human beings can even conceive of such things is phenomenal, although perhaps no less phenomenal than our ability to conceive of God. What is harder to believe: that we live in an expanding universe so vast that light from the frontier takes more than twice the age of the earth to reach our telescopes,[10] or that within, beyond, and throughout this vastness there is a compassionate deity who knows each of us by name?

If nothing else, reading a little cosmology now and then is a good corrective for those of us who speak too easily of God. If we really believe the one whom we worship is the creator of heaven and earth, then where do we get the nerve to offer tidy explanations about exactly who that one is and exactly how that one acts? What allows us to believe that our language is adequate, and what can explain our shocking lack of respect? If we could actually feel ourselves sliding through space at the rate of six hundred thirty kilometers per second, would we still pester God about good weather for the family reunion or the new members drive at church?

The truth is that we have been given a way to approach the God who passes all understanding. Through the miracle of the incarnation, we have been given a revelation of our place in the cosmos. It is a central place, which is only surprising if you forget what the universe remembers: that all places were once the same place, back when all times were one time.

In this revelation, heaven and earth form a unity. So do body and soul. Any apparent division between the two is a temporary illusion, the effect of looking through a dim glass that will not always be there. One day it will vanish, and the clear view will go on forever. Meanwhile, we know enough to know what we do not know, and that in itself is a marvel.

While science might prefer to use the word "discovery" instead of "revelation," the scientific establishment is no less amazed by our ability to know things. The best example is the domain of mathematics, which is pure thought. Einstein's special theory of relativity did not begin with his observation of something funny going on in the real world. It began with a thought experiment as he pondered the question, "What would I see if I were to chase a beam of light at the velocity of light?" His answer involved covering a chalkboard with chalk before he came up with the mathematical equation: $E = MC^2$. In simplest terms, what the math asserts is that matter is frozen energy.

The amazing thing is that his equation worked. The mathematical pattern in Einstein's head matched an actual pattern in the physical world. Pure thought lined up perfectly with real matter, leading Einstein to say that the only incomprehensible thing about the universe is that it is comprehensible.[11] Through us, the cosmos knows itself. Because we are here to think it and say it, the universe is conscious of itself in a way it might not otherwise be. There are limits to our knowledge, certainly, but the fact that we are able to know anything at all is a thoroughly underrated miracle.

> When I look at your heavens,
>   the work of your fingers,
>   the moon and the stars that you
>   have established;
> what are human beings
>   that you are mindful of them,
>   mortals that you care for them?
> Yet you have made them a little
>   lower than God,
> and crowned them with glory and honor.
>   (Psalm 8. 3-5)

One of the hardest things for a believer in God to accept about science is the role that randomness seems to play. According to the classical model of evolution, we are here by sheer chance. If creation could be rewound and played all over again, it is not likely that anything remotely resembling us would emerge twice in a row. In theoretical quantum physics, Heisenberg's uncertainty principle gets at the same thing. Until it is observed, a particle hangs in quantum limbo with all its possibilities intact. When an observer collapses the probability wave, the odds are as good that the particle will turn out one way as another.

This substitution of probabilities for facts was Einstein's chief objection to quantum mechanics. "God does not play dice," he said. Furthermore, he wrote to a friend, if it turned out that God did, then he would rather be "a cobbler, or even an employee in a gaming-house, than a physicist."[12]

Randomness has never appealed to humankind. For those who are religious, it is an affront to faith in an intelligent creator, who made the world by design. For those who are not religious, it is an affront to human genius, which prides itself on the discernment of order. What unites both groups is the hope that the apparent randomness is no more than a temporary hiatus in human knowledge, a kind of riddle that will surely — very soon — be solved.

A man named Edward Lorenz exemplified this hope. He was not a physicist. He was a research meteorologist at the Massachusetts Institute of Technology in the 1960s, working on a Royal McBee computer that chugged along about as fast as a riding mower. Lorenz was passionate about weather the way some men are passionate about fly-fishing. He wanted to solve its mysteries. He wanted to map the variables and come up with patterns that would help him predict the future. If astronomers could pinpoint the return of Haley's comet from seventy-six years away, he reasoned, then he should be able to predict the weather in New York City a mere month ahead of time.

In order to do that, he had to figure out how weather patterns changed over time, which the Royal McBee allowed him to do. Through trial and error, he came up with twelve mathematical equations to govern his computer universe (three times as many as Newton, incidentally, due to scientific inflation?). They were the same rules he saw operating in the real world, defining the relationship between temperature and barometric pressure, between pressure and wind speed.

He plugged them into his computer and let the system go. Piles and piles of printouts stacked up, on which Lorenz could watch the weather patterns develop. The air stream swung north, then south. The pressure rose and fell. He could see the patterns, but he could never make them repeat themselves, not exactly. When he plugged in the same variables they produced different results, leading him deeper and deeper into the mystery.

Finally, one day in the winter of 1961, he took a shortcut. He wanted to look at one part of one sequence in more detail, but he did not want to start the whole run all over again from the beginning. So he started it in the middle instead, giving the machine its initial conditions by typing the numbers straight from an earlier printout. Then he went down the hall for a cup of coffee.

When he came back, Lorenz found a weather pattern so different from the one before that there was no resemblance between the two. He checked his numbers. He checked the vacuum tubes in the computer. Then he realized what had happened. One of the numbers he was working with was .506127. At least that was the number stored in the computer's memory. To save space, the number on the printout was rounded off to .506, and that was the number Lorenz had typed in. He had assumed that the difference between the two — .000127 — was inconsequential, but that was where he was wrong.

That tiny number, way down in the thousandths — as far as the weather was concerned, a puff of wind no bigger than a baby's sneeze or the beat of a butterfly's wings — that tiny little change at the beginning of a weather system turned out to be the difference between a blue sky and a monsoon. Lorenz' discovery was the beginning of a new science — the science of chaos — which, along with relativity and quantum physics, provided the third great revolution in physical science this century.

Simply put, chaos theory tells us why you can break a rack of pool balls exactly the same way and get a different result every time. Even if you had a machine that could regulate your aim and strength, you would get a different result every time, because the tiniest changes in the environment at the beginning of your stroke — not only something as close as your partner's hiccup but also something as far away as the gravitational pull of an electron at the far edge of the Milky Way[13] — just .000127 of a change is the difference between Willie Mosconi's triple bank shot and a cue ball in the pocket.

So that is the bad news about chaos theory, but you knew it all along. Life is not predictable. Furthermore, it never will be, no matter how kind, conscientious, careful, and organized you are. The difference between a blue sky and a monsoon may be as infinitesimal as a cat hair that works its way under your contact lens while you are trying to pass a truck on the expressway, or one lung cell that suddenly blossoms into cancer. Chaos is the name of the game. However strong the illusion of order may be, there is an essential messiness to life that cannot be controlled.

The good news about chaos is that there is an apparent boundary to it. What Edward Lorenz discovered on his Royal McBee and what scores of scientists after him have confirmed is that even though chaotic systems never behave the same way twice and are therefore unpredictable, there is an outer limit beyond which they will not go. Lorenz' computer-generated weather patterns never repeated themselves, it is true, but they never ran off the page either. When he mapped their constantly changing variables, what he came up with was a beautiful double spiral in three dimensions, like the eyes of a hoot owl or the wings of butterfly. No two lines ever repeated themselves on that map, but over time they traced a pattern no one could miss. Named a "strange attractor," it is a picture of the elegant order that underlies chaos. What it tells us is that no matter how random things may seem, how crazy and out of control, there is a hidden symmetry in them, "like a face peering from behind clouds."[14]

You may make of this what you will. As far as I am concerned, you may call it physics or you may call it God. If you call it God, then "strange attractor" may not be the language you use. You may prefer the language of Matthew or Luke, both of whom quote Jesus as saying something like this: "Are not two sparrows sold for a penny? Yet not one of them will fall to the ground apart from your Father. And even the hairs of your head are all counted. So do not be afraid; you are of more value than many sparrows" (Matthew 10.29-31).

Whatever language you prefer, the apparent truth is that we belong to a web of creation in which nothing, absolutely nothing, is inconsequential. The hairs of your head, a baby's sneeze, the gravitational pull of an electron at the far edge of the Milky Way—none of these things is negligible. Not one of them can be subtracted from creation, *or even rounded off,* without changing the whole gorgeous geometry of the universe. Day by day, we may not be able to measure their effect, but that does not seem to bother them. They just go on doing their jobs, helping to lay down the patterns that give shape to our lives.

Every one of us will change the world, whether we mean to or not. All it takes is .000127. Shift anything in the world that much and you may be the catalyst that turns a monsoon into a blue sky (or the other way around). Pick up some stranger's crying baby at exactly the right moment and that baby may turn out to be an artist instead of a tyrant. Cough at the wrong moment and you may make someone lose a game of pool on Mars. You just never know.

All you know for sure is that your best-laid plans are susceptible to chaos, and—conversely—that what looks to you like the worst kind of chaos is really a beautiful double spiral in three dimensions. Whatever else you have faith in, have faith in this: there is a strange attractor at work in your life that will not let you fly off the page. There is no order without chaos. There is no chaos without order. They give birth to each other, again and again.

As a metaphor, chaos theory raises all sorts of interesting questions for religion. Is the future open or closed? Does the freedom God has granted us include the freedom to affect how things will turn out, or is the end point set and our only problem how to get there? Is life a journey or a dance?

Earlier in this century, while Albert Einstein was working on his relativity theories, the British mathematician and philosopher Alfred North Whitehead was developing his process philosophy, which attempts to answer such questions. Those who are interested may try to find a copy of his 1929 classic, *Process and Reality: An Essay in Cosmology,* or later volumes by his theological heirs Charles Hartshorne and John Cobb, Jr. Those who do not wish to go to so much trouble may simply consult their Bibles, where God is said to "repent" (Exodus 32.14) and to discover things God had not known about what humans might do (Genesis 22.12).

My friendly critics have raised the question of a "God of the gaps." Both science and religion have been guilty of using "God" as a synonym for "that which we do not understand." The danger in that is that science gets to determine how big God is, forcing God to retreat further and further into the regions of the unknown as science extends the boundaries of the known. Rather than invoking God only when natural explanations fail, it may make more sense to understand God as the God not of facts but of meaning. This would excuse religion from the doomed enterprise of trying to explain the undiscovered and unknown, and free its energy for the discernment and communication of meaning. However far human beings turn out to be from the center of the universe, we remain at the center of the generation of meaning.

Meanwhile, there are realms of human experience that science can never address, since they do not yield themselves to mathematical equation or empirical verification. There are also people whose lives are no better for all the science in the world. As Mark Helprin wrote in a recent essay, "If salvation depends on development and advancement, what does that imply about the lame, the weak, the befuddled, and the oppressed?"[15] And yet a dialogue between science and religion offers each discipline a check on its hubris. While science disputes religion's certainty that purpose is built into creation, religion challenges science's certainty that such purpose is impossible.

Whether the subject is cosmology or theology, chaos theory or prayer, there are limits to our knowledge. Science cannot explain where complexity comes from any better than religion can explain why bad things happen to good people. Every effort to understand reality begins with a leap of faith: the acceptance of a certain point of view, the adoption of a certain set of symbols. Whichever ones we choose, there does not, at this moment in time, seem to be any way around the experience of awe.

According to Albert Einstein, "The most beautiful emotion we can experience is the mystical. It is the source of all true art and science. He to whom this emotion is a stranger, who can no longer wonder and stand rapt in awe, is as good as dead." Teilhard de Chardin, the Jesuit paleontologist, said, "Less and less do I see any difference between research and adoration."

One Fourth of July I stood on the bank of the East River along with most of the rest of New York City and watched the sky explode with light. There were fireworks that opened like flowers, with green blossoming into blue that spit out spores of white. There were red hearts that grew larger as they flew toward us. There were triple-tiered fountains of gold that spilled silver stars. The sky was so bright that all the people in front of me were no more than dark silhouettes. About ten feet away, a child sat on her father's shoulders. Every time there was a new explosion in the sky, she reached her right hand toward it, trying to curl her fingers around the light. She did this over and over again, so that all my memories of those vastly different fireworks have the same small dark hand in them, reaching for the sky.

As far as I know, she never caught a single spark, but neither did she ever stop trying.

Endnotes

I. Between Science and Faith

1. Kenneth L. Woodward, "How the Heavens Go," *Newsweek* (July 20, 1998), 52.

2. Edward J. Larson and Larry Witham, "Scientists and Religion in America," *Scientific American* (September 1999), 88-93.

3. Ibid., 91.

4. Stephen W. Hawking, *A Brief History of Time* (New York: Bantam Books, 1988), 175.

5. Margie Wylie, "Should robots be baptized?" *Mobile Register* (September 25, 1999).

6. George Johnson, "Space-Time: The Final Frontier," a review of *The Elegant Universe* by Brian Greene in *The New York Times Book Review* (February 21, 1999), 6.

7. Lee Adams Young, http://www.scienceandfaith.org/physI/heisenberg6a.htm.

8. Richard Dawkins, "Snake Oil and Holy Water," *Forbes ASAP* (October 4, 1999), 236.

9. Richard P. Feynman, *The Meaning of It All* (Reading, Mass.: Addison-Wesley, 1998), 28.

II. The Evolution of Praise

1. Edward B. Davis, "Debating Darwin: The 'intelligent design' movement," *The Christian Century* (July 15-22, 1998), 681.

2. Walter Wink, *The Powers That Be* (New York: Doubleday, 1998), 45.

3. George Johnson, *Fire in the Mind* (New York: Vintage Books, 1995), 35.

4. Jared Diamond, "Evolving Backward," *Discover* (September 1998), 64-65.

5. Michael D. Lemonick and Andrea Dorfman, "Up From the Apes," *Time* (August 23, 1999), 52.

6. Johnson, *Fire in the Mind*, 245.

7. Timothy Ferris, *Coming of Age in the Milky Way* (New York: Anchor Books/Doubleday, 1988), 100.

8. Retold by Timothy Ferris in *The Whole Shebang* (New York: Simon & Schuster, 1997), 292.

9. Fred Hoyle, "The Universe: Past and Present Reflections," *Engineering & Science* (November 1981), 12.

10. Quoted in Ferris, *The Whole Shebang,* 305-306.

11. Bennett J. Sims, *Servanthood* (Cambridge, Mass.: Cowley Publications, 1997), 175.

12. Johnson, *Fire in the Mind,* 269.

13. Ibid.

14. Paul Davies, *Superforce: The Search for a Grand Unified Theory of Nature* (London: Unwin, 1985), 192.

15. Ferris, *The Whole Shebang*, 32.

16. Sidney Liebes, Elisabeth Sahtouris, and Brian Swimme, *A Walk Through Time* (New York: Wiley, 1998), 18.

17. Denis Edwards, *Made from Stardust* (North Blackburn, Victoria, Australia: CollinsDove, 1992), 41.

18. See http://www.cosmiccommode.com/, with thanks to Tom McMullen for the lead.

19. Ferris, *Coming of Age in the Milky Way*, 214.

20. Ferris, *The Whole Shebang*, 20.

21. Ibid., 178.

22. Edwards, *Made from Stardust*, 42.

23. Ibid., 43.

24. Johnson, *Fire in the Mind*, 222.

25. Arthur Peacocke, *God and the New Biology* (London: J. M. Dent and Sons, 1986), 129.

III. The Physics of Communion

1. "The Unspeakable Things That Particles Do," *The New York Times* (July 27, 1997), 5.

2. Johnson, *Fire in the Mind*, 52.

3. Ibid., 146.

4. Richard Elliott Friedman, *The Disappearance of God* (Boston: Little, Brown, 1995), 222.

5. "Science Sees The Light," *The New Republic* (October 12, 1998), 28.

6. John North, *The Norton History of Astronomy and Cosmology* (New York: W. W. Norton, 1995), 67.

7. Ferris, *Coming of Age in the Milky Way*, 42.

8. Ibid., 67.

9. Kenneth L. Woodward, "How The Heavens Go," *Newsweek* (July 20, 1998), 52.

10. Ferris, *Coming of Age in the Milky Way,* 100.

11. Ibid., 121.

12. My thanks to Alan Watts for this image (from his lecture "Coincidence of Opposites" in volume I of "The Tao of Philosophy" audiocassette series, produced in 1973 by the Electronic University (Box 2309, San Anselmo, CA 94979).

13. Alain Aspect, "Bell's inequality test: more ideal than ever," *Nature* (March 18, 1999), 189.

14. Ferris, *The Whole Shebang,* 277.

15. Paul Davies, *God and the New Physics* (New York: Simon & Schuster, 1983), 162-163.

16. Margaret J. Wheatley, *Leadership and the New Science* (San Francisco: Berrett-Koehler, 1992), 4.

17. Ibid., 31.

18. My thanks to Dr. Louis K. Jensen for these metaphors.

19. Davies, *God and the New Physics,* 112.

20. John Polkinghorne, *Quarks, Chaos and Christianity* (New York: Crossroad, 1997), 112.

21. Ibid., 82-83.

22. Ferris, *The Whole Shebang,* 283.

23. Ibid., 284.

24. Ibid., 287.

IV. The Limits of Knowledge

1. Abraham Pais, *Niels Bohr's Times in Physics, Philosophy, and Polity* (Oxford: Clarendon Press, 1991), 439.

2. Fred Alan Wolf, *Taking the Quantum Leap* (New York: Harper & Row, 1989), 117.

3. Sharon Begley, "Science Finds God," *Newsweek* (July 20, 1998), 51.

4. Fenton Johnson, "Beyond Belief," *Harper's Magazine* (September 1998), 40.

5. Polkinghorne, *Quarks, Chaos and Christianity*, 5.

6. Johnson, *Fire in the Mind*, 121.

7. Ibid., 175.

8. Ferris, *The Whole Shebang*, 121.

9. Ibid., 131.

10. Ibid., 11.

11. Polkinghorne, *Quarks, Chaos and Christianity*, 24.

12. Ferris, *Coming of Age in the Milky Way*, 290.

13. Johnson, *Fire in the Mind*, 94.

14. Ibid., 96.

15. "Contrivance," *Forbes ASAP* (October 4, 1999), 250.

Recommended Reading

Barbour, Ian G. *Religion and Science: Historical and Contemporary Issues.* San Francisco: Harper SanFrancisco, 1997.

Bohm, David. *On Dialogue.* New York: Routledge, 1996.

Davies, Paul. *The Mind of God: The Scientific Basis for a Rational World.* New York: Simon & Schuster, 1992.

— — —. *God and the New Physics.* New York: Simon & Schuster, 1983.

Edwards, Denis. *Made from Stardust: Exploring the Place of Human Beings Within Creation.* North Blackburn, Victoria, Australia: CollinsDove, 1992.

Eiseley, Loren. *The Star Thrower.* New York: Harcourt Brace Jovanovich, 1978.

Ferris, Timothy. *Coming of Age in the Milky Way.* New York: Anchor Books/Doubleday, 1988.

— — —. *The Whole Shebang: A State of the Universe Report.* New York: Simon & Schuster, 1997.

Feynman, Richard P. *The Meaning of It All: Thoughts of a Citizen-Scientist.* Reading, Mass.: Addison-Wesley, 1998.

Gleick, James. *Chaos.* New York: Penguin, 1988.

Goodwin, Brian. *How the Leopard Changed Its Spots: The Evolution of Complexity.* New York: Charles Scribner's Sons, 1994.

Greene, Brian. *The Elegant Universe: Superstrings, Hidden Dimensions, and the Quest for the Ultimate Theory.* New York: W. W. Norton & Company, 1999.

Johnson, George. *Fire in the Mind: Science, Faith, and the Search for Order.* New York: Vintage Books, 1995.

Larson, Edward J. *Summer for the Gods: The Scopes Trial and America's Continuing Debate over Science and Religion.* New York: Basic Books, 1997.

Liebes, Sidney, Elisabeth Sahtouris, and Brian Swimme. *A Walk Through Time: From Stardust to Us.* New York: John Wiley & Sons, 1998.

Lindberg, David C. and Ronald L. Numbers, eds. *God and Nature: Historical Essays on the Encounter between Christianity and Science.* Berkeley: University of California Press, 1986.

McFague, Sallie. *The Body of God: An Ecological Theology.* Minneapolis: Fortress Press, 1993.

North, John. *The Norton History of Astronomy and Cosmology.* New York: W. W. Norton & Company, 1995.

Pannenberg, Wolfhart. *Towards a Theology of Nature.* Louisville, Kentucky: Westminster/John Knox Press, 1993.

Peacocke, Arthur. *God and the New Biology.* London: J. M. Dent and Sons, 1986.

— — —. *Theology for a Scientific Age: Being and Becoming – Natural, Divine and Human.* Minneapolis: Fortress Press, 1993.

Polkinghorne, John. *Belief in God in an Age of Science.* New Haven: Yale University Press, 1998.

— — —. *The Faith of a Physicist: Reflections of a Bottom-Up Thinker.* Princeton: Princeton University Press, 1994.

— — —. *Quarks, Chaos and Christianity.* New York: Crossroad, 1994.

Teilhard de Chardin, Pierre. *The Phenomenon of Man.* New York: Harper, 1959.

Wentzel van Huyssteen, J. *Duet or Duel? Theology and Science in a Postmodern World.* Harrisburg, Penn.: Trinity Press International, 1998.

Wheatley, Margaret J. *Leadership and the New Science.* San Francisco: Berrett-Koehler Publishers, 1992.

Cowley Publications is a ministry of the Society of St. John the Evangelist, a religious community for men in the Episcopal Church. Emerging from the Society's tradition of prayer, theological reflection, and diversity of mission, the press is centered in the rich heritage of the Anglican Communion.

Cowley Publications seeks to provide books, audio cassettes, and other resources for the ongoing theological exploration and spiritual development of the Episcopal Church and others in the body of Christ. To this end, it is dedicated to developing a new generation of theological writers, encouraging them to produce timely, creative, and stimulating publications of excellence, and making these publications available widely, reaching both clergy and lay persons.